EMPLOYEE DEVELOPMENT
ON A SHOESTRING

EMPLOYEE DEVELOPMENT ON A SHOESTRING

Halelly Azulay

ASTD PRESS

Alexandria, Virginia

ASTD Press is an internationally renowned source of insightful and practical information on workplace learning and performance topics, including training basics, evaluation and return on investment, instructional systems development, e-learning, leadership, and career development. Visit us at www.astd.org/astdpress.

Ordering information: Books published by ASTD Press can be purchased by visiting our website at store.astd.org or by calling 800.628.2783 or 703.683.8100.

Library of Congress Control Number: 2012930634
ISBN-10: 1-56286-800-4
ISBN-13: 978-1-56286-800-0

ASTD Press Editorial Staff:
Director: Anthony Allen
Senior Manager, Production & Editorial: Glenn Saltzman
Project Manager, Content Acquisition: Kristin Husak
Associate Editor: Heidi Smith
Editorial, Design, and Production: Abella Publishing Services, LLC
Cover Design: Ana Ilieva Foreman
Printed by: Versa Press, Inc., East Peoria, IL, www.versapress.com

CONTENTS

Chapter 2. Flying Solo: Self-Directed Learning

Chapter 3. Doing Good: Learning by Volunteering

Chapter 6. Move and Stretch: Learning Through Rotational and Stretch Assignments

Chapter 7. Team Effort: Learning in Special Teams

Chapter 8. Teaching to Learn: Learning by Teaching Others

Chapter 9. Fun and Games: Learning via Games and Contests

Chapter 10. Digital Storytelling: Learning by Creating Videos and Podcasts

Chapter 11. Zoning Out: Learning Through Innovation/Creativity Zones

Chapter 12. Getting Social: Social Learning Tools

Summary—Now What?

FOREWORD

Developing employees is "job one," to paraphrase an American carmaker. And that "job one" belongs to supervisors.

As Halelly points out in the introduction, it is estimated that 70 percent of leadership development takes place through informal learning as opposed to formal learning events. More learning probably occurs in the break room than the classroom, and more skills may be learned from a co-worker than an instructor. Think about your own experiences. You probably learn more by accident than intentionally. If this is the case, supervisors can be more deliberate about how employees learn to ensure that they are as productive as possible. Supervisors (and employees as well) need to intentionally seek out not only what they need to learn, but also how they will learn. Supervisors can enhance this critical part of their jobs by consciously creating informal developmental opportunities for their employees. Halelly shows you how.

Numerous alternatives exist for informal development. As a supervisor, consider which learning strategies and developmental assignments you wish to use and why. The biggest advantage of informal learning is that each experience can be customized for the needs of the learner. This isn't usually the case with classroom or online training. Four considerations help guide your choices.

Honor your employees. Starting with their individual development plans (IDPs), consider what your employees know, what they are proficient at, and what they need to experience in both their current and future jobs. Factor in their learning styles as well. For example, you may not want to assign the shyest person in your department the task of designing a brown-bag presentation as a first informal learning experience.

Build in variety. Just because you had a great experience as a protégé does not mean that a mentoring experience is necessary for every employee. As you consider variety, match the need-to-know with the how-to-learn. For example, someone who needs to learn to communicate better will do better with a team assignment than reading a communication book.

Seek what's natural. Identify developmental experiences that arise naturally from the employee's work or departmental needs. Do you have an employee who needs experience leading a team? Does your department need to solve a workflow problem? Perhaps you can address both existing issues with one developmental assignment. When an assignment solves a naturally existing need, everyone benefits.

Finally, *multiply your results.* Identify one developmental opportunity that addresses numerous learning needs for the same individual. For example, if you have an employee who is uncomfortable with ambiguity, is a loner, and needs to learn to work as part of a team, a start-up assignment could address several of this employee's needs.

You will not read long before Halelly's ideas begin to inspire you to action. She offers a compendium of resources and tools to help supervisors carry out "job one." She has included almost a dozen developmental method chapters, and inside each chapter you will find dozens of specific ideas including worksheets, self-assessments, developmental planning sheets, goal-setting formats, case studies, and other time-saving tools.

Many of the ideas presented in this book allow employees to learn and develop skills while maintaining their current jobs. These are options for developing that are in place. Working on start-up projects, leading process improvement teams, designing brown-bag or other learning sessions, integrating temporary assignments, and conducting research online are examples of assignments that allow employees to develop practical skills in place, while also maintaining their current responsibilities.

Your employees' IDPs identify specific developmental goals. I try to ratchet those goals up a notch by taking a more comprehensive perspective. I try to think in terms of broader developmental enhancement that also encompasses the IDP-required competencies (such as delegating or managing conflict). For example, I might pose these questions:

- What experiences will benefit this employee in terms of working in a broader scope that involves multiple locations, products, services, or functions, while at the same time developing required competencies?
- What external interfaces with groups such as customers, unions, partners, suppliers, or regulatory agencies will be helpful to this employee?
- How can I reshape this employee's job responsibilities so that she has more experience planning for the future?
- What responsibilities is this employee likely to face in her next job that she is not familiar with today?
- How can I provide this individual with experiences that involve working across cultures?
- What management skills could be developed in a non-work setting?

Responding to these kinds of questions adds a different dimension and depth to employees' learning experiences. As a supervisor, you can provide an opportunity for your employee to gain competencies and, at the same time, provide the employee with a broader set of developmental experiences.

Of the respondents in a 2011 *Human Resource Executive* magazine survey of 800 HR executives, 84 percent stated that they were concerned about losing talent as an economic recovery takes hold. Second only to increasing communication, respondents stated that they will "provide employees with additional training and development" to boost retention. Whether you are concerned with retaining talent, increasing productivity, or ensuring that your employees have the expertise they need to get the job done, the ideas in this book will engage your employees in practical learning experiences and demonstrate that you have their developmental interests in mind.

According to the American Society for Training and Development (ASTD) *2010 State of the Industry Report*, U.S. companies spend $126 billion annually on employee learning and development programs. As you decide how you will invest your organization's portion of that $126 billion, think about expanding your options. If you have always assigned reading or cross-functional teamwork, try setting up a rotational assignment or assigning someone to develop a podcast. You will find it rewarding as you branch out and identify new ways for your employees to learn.

Developing in place on the job is an unfamiliar concept to many of the supervisors with whom I work. They continue to think of traditional learning options—classes most often—as the only way to develop employees. However, once I suggest other ideas, they quickly understand the benefits and think of their own learning options and ideas for their own employees. Often these ideas come directly from the supervisors' to-do lists.

Whether you are a supervisor looking for "job one" developmental ideas or a trainer seeking ways to stretch your company's training and development budget, this book delivers. Halelly introduces you to the concepts to begin your employee development journey; she lays out the route to ensure a smooth ride; she presents tips, assessments, and worksheets to guide your trip; and in the end, you will reach your destination with the wisdom and excitement to traverse this trail again. Use this book to develop your employees. Depend on this book to guide your own supervisory development.

October 2011
Elaine Biech
ebb associates inc
Editor, *The ASTD Leadership Handbook*
Author, *The Business of Consulting*

INTRODUCTION

Why This Book?

When I first told my husband about the idea for this book, he responded, "You mean, you're going to write yourself out of a job?" Why would someone who makes her living facilitating learning, often in a classroom or a formal learning program, try to help supervisors, HR and training professionals, and employees find ways to develop skills outside the classroom and without her help?

Well, I don't think this book will put the training industry out of business. Far from it. I wrote this book because I am passionate about learning and development. I wrote this book because I am passionate about supporting leaders in their efforts to become more effective. And I wrote this book because often, training is simply not the answer.

It is estimated that 70 percent of all leadership development takes place via on-the-job experiences rather than formal learning events. The "70-20-10 rule," as this idea has become known, says that development happens in three ways: 70 percent on-the-job experience, 20 percent through relationships and feedback, and 10 percent from formal training opportunities [traced back to research by the Center for Creative Leadership, published first in *The Lessons of Experience* (McCall, Lombardo, and Morrison, 1988)].

All over the world, supervisors and professionals like you are faced with a challenging task of helping their staff members grow and develop within limited budgets and timelines and ever-increasing pressures to perform more with less. Supervisors and employees desperately need alternatives and complements to the usual approach, because it is not enough. And many of you are so overwhelmed with a growing workload that you simply don't have the time or the requisite knowledge to come up with creative ideas for developing skills within the parameters that are presented to you.

Well, this book is here to help.

You don't have to spend any time searching for ideas, because they're right here in this book. You don't have to spend time thinking up possible obstacles to each method—I've done that for you. And you don't have to spend lots of time designing implementation plans because I've created the tools and supports to help you quickly ensure that your employee development methods are successful and sustainable.

Who Can Benefit From Reading This Book?

The book is written primarily to address the needs of those in a position to help employees develop in their current jobs. Whether you are a supervisor, a manager, a director, or an executive, a key part of your role ("job one" as Elaine Biech puts it in her foreword) is to ensure that employees are growing and learning. If you are a talent management, human resource, personnel, talent development, training, organization development, or workplace learning professional, your job is to ensure that supervisors throughout your organization are tending to this "job one." Perhaps you are a mentor or career counselor or coach, and you are using this book to help your protégé or client make career development plans. And if you are a self-motivated, self-starting employee, you may enjoy reading this book to get ideas about how to take your development into your own hands rather than waiting for others to suggest strategies to you. Anyone who wants to ensure that employees are developing new skills and knowledge and who realizes that sending them to a training class cannot be, and should not be, the only path to achieve that outcome, should read and benefit from the ideas presented in this book.

How Should You Use This Book?

This book can be used by anyone, anywhere. It contains lots of different ideas about a variety of employee development methods because every workplace is different, every budget is different, and every employee developer has a different level of availability or interest. I've grouped the chapters in order of the probable ease with which you can implement each of the employee development methods. Always start with the prerequisite goal setting and preparation chapter, regardless of the employee development method you choose, and use the many templates, worksheets, and checklists offered there to get you ready and focused on the right path and in the right direction.

The rest of the chapters are loosely ordered by ease of implementation or level of organizational support requirements: from easy to implement, to moderate implementation difficulty, and finally to those employee development methods that need greater effort and support. But take note: Just about every method can be implemented in a way that makes it easier and more effortless than the "typical" approach, and vice versa. The methods are not interdependent. Each chapter is a universe unto itself, and the order is just a general suggestion. I encourage you to scan the titles and skip around to those that strike your fancy, or that seem easiest to apply or most fitting for your workplace and employee needs.

By describing a wide range of independent options, it is my hope that you find a few that seem to fit your needs at this moment and begin implementing them immediately. You can start where you are right now and work up from there. Then, when those initial methods are implemented successfully, you can come back to the book, learn about other methods, and apply them as you and your organization become ready. It's the book that keeps on giving.

Bottom line: There is no wrong order to read this book—you can chart your own path!

How Is This Book Structured?

As I mentioned in the previous section, the book can be read in any order you want after you read chapter 1. Some readers will enjoy reading it in linear order, from start to finish. Others may like to jump around based on those chapter topics that seem most attractive, or most unusual, or most actionable to them. Maybe you read and implement three methods of employee development first. Then, you might come back once those methods are in place and learn a couple more ideas that you can implement and grow your offerings for employee development. And maybe some of the chapters just appeal intellectually, and you are not able to put them into practice in your current organization, but you might use them down the road, in your next opportunity in another organization or environment. However you choose to read it, here's what's in store for you in this book.

In chapter 1, "Ready, Set, Aim! Goal Setting and Preparation," you will be reminded of some important principles for setting good development goals, such as identifying the learner's readiness, crafting goals that are SMART, and identifying the right competencies on which you want to zero in. In addition, you can make the business case for each development method and plan its implementation using checklists and templates.

In the first part of the book, "easy to implement" methods are the focus. Chapter 2 introduces self-directed learning ideas that are simple to implement and take into account the learner's preferred learning style. Chapter 3, "Doing Good: Learning by Volunteering," presents the idea that employees can develop a variety of skills outside their work environment for no cost to the organization when they take on volunteer jobs in industry and community organizations. Chapter 4 describes how taking a learning sabbatical could be a wonderful way to create intense immersion in a development approach that lasts between four weeks and six months or even a year, depending on the situation. The last chapter in this "easy to implement" part is chapter 5, which introduces mentoring as a learning modality that many employees can benefit from, whether they serve as the protégé or the mentor in the relationship.

After chapter 5, the employee development methods involve moderate implementation difficulty. Chapter 6 introduces learning through rotational and stretch assignments that allows employees to either take a temporary break from their current jobs or become involved in an assignment while continuing their usual work. In either case, the assignment allows the employees to stretch outside their comfort zones to grow their skills. Special teams, discussed in chapter 7, offer an opportunity to stretch skills while learning to work with others, usually from across the organization. Serving on such teams provides employees an opportunity to contribute to the organization by working on a special problem or creating process improvement opportunities, all while still performing their usual work duties. Chapter 8 focuses on learning by teaching others, especially within the employee's organization. It is often said that the best way to learn something is to teach it.

Finally, in the last group of chapters, we take a look at some employee development methods that may require a bit more effort and organizational support or resources. In chapter 9, we see how learning can be served as a game or a contest that engages employees while building up morale and tapping into people's natural desire for playfulness and friendly competition. Chapter 10 focuses on "Digital Storytelling: Learning by Creating Videos and Podcasts," which creates an opportunity for any employee to create and upload learning content for others in the organization to enjoy. The process of developing videos and podcasts is a richly developmental one, and presents a win-win for the organization. Chapter 11 presents a novel idea of creating innovation/creativity zones that push employees to think outside the box and outside their regular job duties for a specific period or portion of time, either for a one-off event or in a recurring pattern (such as for 10 or 20 percent of every week or month). And chapter 12 rounds out the employee development method ideas by presenting the many developmental opportunities created with the introduction (and ongoing development) of various social learning tools that allow employees to learn and connect online with experts and peers across the enterprise, in real time and as their development needs arise.

The book closes with a summary that ties together all the ideas and challenges you to move from ideas to implementation so that you can create a robust, diverse employee development plan for each employee that goes beyond the tried-and-true classroom and online training methodology, as well as maximizes your development budget and employee engagement at the same time.

Acknowledgments

My heart is filled with gratitude for many who have helped, guided, or inspired me along my path to writing this book.

First and foremost, to my best friend, life partner, and amazing husband, David, for believing in me and supporting me, always. Your love sustained me through the rough spots and soared with me during the highs. And to my talented, creative, funny, and wise boys, Tal and Guy, for cheering me on and bearing with me when I disappeared to write for days at a time. Helping you learn and grow is an incredible and rewarding responsibility. I love you all very much.

To my incredible parents, Sol and Batia, for always pushing me to be my best and loving me as I am, for being my best friends, and for sharing their highest values with me. I can't believe how lucky I was to be born to you.

To my brother Yovi, my sister-in-law Lian, and their sweet Luca and Geffen, for the laughter and friendship. To my brother Ron and sister-in-law Nefrit for their support and encouragement. I'm so glad you are my family!

To good friends who have encouraged, supported, and inspired me along the writing journey: Limor Hasson, Rewital Schneider-Chashper, Orit Greenberg, Howard Walper, Wendy Mack, and Kathryn Gaines.

To writers Diane Elkins, Kathy Reiffenstein, Darlene Christopher, Karen Mack, Kevin Nourse, Kathryn Gaines, and Marissa Levin for their fellowship.

To authors and writers Ayn Rand, David Allen, Daniel Pink, Mark Levy, Brian "CopyBlogger" Clark, Caroline Adams Miller (whom I'm lucky to also count as a friend), Mihály Csíkszentmihályi, and Marcus Buckingham for inspiring and teaching me.

To my trainer Judd Borokove and his crew at CrossFit Bethesda, for making me do more burpees, pull-ups, and all manner of other challenging exercises to keep in shape while conceiving of and writing the book.

To Justin Brusino at ASTD Press for buying into the concept, bringing me into the ASTD Press family, and guiding me through the manuscript development process. To Kristin Husak and Heidi Smith at ASTD Press for helping with the final transition from development to production. And to the tireless ASTD Press Production and Editorial staff—Abella Publishing Services' Belinda Thresher, Melinda Masson, and others—who took the raw material I provided and made it into a beautiful, coherent, marketable product.

To the case study contributors Michelle Moore, Justin Suissa, Mirna Phillips, Jack Teuber, Shannon Schuyler, Cindy Huggett,

Manuel Figallo, Dr. Terri Paluszkiewicz, and Adam Zimet, for giving me the opportunity to tell your stories and breathing life into the ideas in this book with your real-life examples.

And to the prolific, talented, wise, inspiring, and generous Elaine Biech, for her mentorship at every step of the way, from the day we brainstormed the initial skeleton idea for the book all the way to honoring me with a foreword to support the success of this book and everything in between. I am truly privileged to count you as a friend.

RESOURCES

McCall, M.W., Jr., M.M. Lombardo, and A.M. Morrison. (1988). *The Lessons of Experience: How Successful Executives Develop on the Job*. New York: Lexington Books.

Chapter 1

READY, SET, AIM! GOAL SETTING AND PREPARATION

Employee development must be a deliberate, planned, and mindful practice. You cannot expect it to be successful if you approach it in a haphazard fashion. Therefore, before you and your employees approach any of the methods described in this book, you need to think about, plan for, and set strong goals, and find the right path to mindfully pursue the accomplishment. Then, use the preparation worksheets, checklists, and templates to ensure that you are on track to successful implementation.

STAGES OF THE DEVELOPMENT PROCESS

How will you set the most appropriate and tailored goals to each employee's developmental level and stage of readiness? Use Table 1-1 to assess the developing employee's personal readiness to develop and commitment to change.

Is the employee at the discovery stage, the development stage, or the demonstration stage? This readiness assessment step is important because if the employee needs to change a behavior but does not yet understand the impact of his actions on others, he will not be able to change this behavior. The employee is simply not ready for that stage of development.

Does the employee need to gain more knowledge and information, more opportunities to practice applying the knowledge or skills, or more opportunities to apply the knowledge and skills effectively on the job?

Table 1-1 ▪ Practical Tool for Assessment of Employees' Readiness for Development and Change

	STAGE	DESCRIPTION OF STAGE
DISCOVERY	1 2 3	Awareness Acceptance Grasping the impact
DEVELOPMENT	4 5 6 7	Desire to improve Understanding (and articulating) the goal Capacity to work on self-improvement Engaging in learning activities
DEMONSTRATION	8 9 10	Practicing the new competency Seeking and accepting feedback and help Demonstrating competence

Once you identify the employee's development needs, another important step is to identify the type of learning that the employee needs to accomplish. What needs to change? Is the gap related to knowledge (the employee doesn't know something), skill (the employee can't do something), attitude (the employee doesn't agree with something), or personal trait (the employee can't be something)? As you can see in Table 1-2, the degree of difficulty for the development goal will increase with each type of learning on this spectrum.

WHAT ARE DEVELOPMENT GOALS?

Goals are broad statements about desired outcomes. They are a way to define your vision of success and the practical path for reaching your desired outcomes. It is important to distinguish between goals and mere activities or tasks. Since goals are the path to your results, they will be broader and grander than tasks on a to-do list. They should focus on the value gained as a result of the behavior, not the behavior itself. You achieve a goal when you attain a specific standard of proficiency on a given task within a specific timeframe. The activities or tasks are the small bites that lead you to accomplish your goals and reach your desired outcomes.

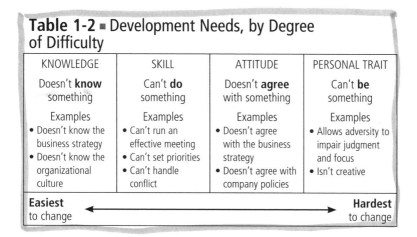

Table 1-2 ■ Development Needs, by Degree of Difficulty

KNOWLEDGE	SKILL	ATTITUDE	PERSONAL TRAIT
Doesn't **know** something	Can't **do** something	Doesn't **agree** with something	Can't **be** something
Examples • Doesn't know the business strategy • Doesn't know the organizational culture	Examples • Can't run an effective meeting • Can't set priorities • Can't handle conflict	Examples • Doesn't agree with the business strategy • Doesn't agree with company policies	Examples • Allows adversity to impair judgment and focus • Isn't creative

Easiest to change ⟵⟶ **Hardest** to change

The development goal or objective should articulate the competency that will be developed, as described later in the chapter, and how the employee's performance will be different. It should focus on the desired performance, or what the individual will be able to do better on the job after completing the development activities, for example: "Develop proficiency in assessing job candidates, resulting in a better match with job requirements and a higher proportion of high-performance or high-potential direct reports, over the next year."

How to Identify Development Goals

Once you identify the employee's readiness and development stage, you'll need to identify learning and development goals for the appropriate kind of employee development effort. What can be expected?

The goals should be specific, measurable, and actionable. "Cindy needs to improve her presentation skills" is vague, general, and hard to envision in its finished state. Instead, phrase the goal as follows: "Cindy is able to deliver a marketing briefing to a senior-level audience that communicates the information in a manner that is clear, concise, and understandable."

Here are some key ingredients of a good goal statement (adapted from Grote, 2002):

* **Active:** Begin with an action verb (*reduce, expand, design, write, increase, create,* and so forth).
* **Key outcome:** Define a key outcome for each goal.
* **Inputs:** Identify inputs that will fuel the goal accomplishment such as costs, materials, equipment, human resources, and time.
* **Success criteria and measures:** How will you know that the goal has been met? How will you measure goal accomplishment?
* **Ownership:** Ensure that the owner of the goal can control the goal.
* **Prioritize:** Compare the goal to your other goals and determine its priority.
* **Track progress:** Determine a way to track progress and get feedback.

Writing SMART Goals

The SMART acronym has been used extensively because it helps guide goal writing in an easily memorable way. Here is a brief description of the letters in SMART:

Specific
Measurable
Aligned
Results-oriented
Time-bound

Specific. A specific goal has a much greater chance of being accomplished than a general goal. Is your goal mutually *understood* and *agreed upon* by you and your manager? The goal should be stated in a straightforward manner and emphasize what you want to happen. Answer the questions: What? Why? and How?

Measurable. Establish concrete *criteria for measuring progress* toward the attainment of each goal you set. Make sure each goal's measures are set at a level that is *high but realistic* (think doable, not easy).

Aligned. Your goal should be aligned with the goals of your department, the goals of your division, and the organization's strategic goals.

Results-oriented. Create goals that will generate visible *outcome-focused* accomplishments. What does each goal deliver? Keep your desired outcomes in mind and explicitly express them in your goals.

Time-bound. Goals are best when *deadlines and milestones* are attached to them. Set a timeframe for the goal: for next quarter, in six months, by year end. Putting an end point on your goal gives you a clear target to work toward. The goals should be *challenging yet attainable*.

> Time-bound goals are inherently more measurable and realistic, and therefore more attainable.

Types of Performance Measures

There are four key types of measures that you can use, separately or in combination:

- *Quality* addresses how well the employee performed the work and the accuracy or effectiveness of the final product. Some concepts related to quality are accuracy, appearance, usefulness, and effectiveness. Quality measures can include error rates and customer satisfaction rates, for example.

> **TIP**
>
> It's best to frame your goal in positive instead of negative terms. Experts found that a negatively framed goal ("Try not to miss more than three of the next 12 meetings") leads to worse performance than a positively framed one ("Try to attend nine or more of the next 12 meetings").
>
> *Source:* Latham (2009).

OBJECTIVE VERSUS SUBJECTIVE MEASURES

We should strive to be objective in our measurement of goal achievement. However, do not assume all *qualitative* measures are inherently *subjective*. Some goals have easily definable quantitative measures, which are clearly superior to qualitative ones *when they are possible*. However, some goals just don't lend themselves to quantitative measures or must have a combination of quantitative and qualitative measures to be complete. It is possible to use qualitative means to judge achievement of a goal and still be objective if the goal is specifically written to address the desired outcomes, and if you and the employee agree about how the goal will be evaluated.

- *Quantity* is a measure of how much work the employee produced. Examples include the number of cases processed, the number of calls taken in an hour, and the number of complaints filed.
- *Timeliness* speaks to how quickly, when, or by what date the work was produced.
- *Cost-effectiveness* relates to monetary savings or cost control. It is a measure of the effective use of resources: human, time, or financial. Examples include adhering to budgets and reducing waste.

Developing Specific Measures

For each goal, consider what general measures are applicable (quality, quantity, timeliness, and cost-effectiveness). Then, ask questions to clarify how you will be able to measure the results more specifically; define the measurement criteria. Some questions might include:

- How can we measure [quality, quantity, and so forth]?
- Is there some number or percent that we can track?
- If no numbers can be measured, how can we judge whether the results are of high quality?
- What factors could we look for to help us judge the effectiveness of the results?
- Is the measurement meaningful?
- Are the numbers within the employee's control?

Use the following example to help you define your goal measures as specifically as possible.

- **Goal:** "Provide guidance and technical assistance to other analysts."

- **General measures:** Quality and timeliness.
- **Specific measures of quality:** "The accuracy of the information provided to other analysts, as determined by the employee's supervisor" and "the perceptions of other analysts that the employee is willing to assist and that her feedback is helpful."
- **Specific measure of timeliness:** "The number of hours it takes for the employee to respond to other analysts' requests for assistance."

Once you identify the development stage for the employee and set SMART goals, you will need to define specific activities to help the employee achieve each goal. Use Table 1-3 (on page 8) to identify some possible development activities that correspond to the employee's goals and development stage.

Examples of Measures for Development Goals

Here are some examples of ways you can measure goal progress both quantitatively and qualitatively.

Quantitative Measures

- Financial impact (for example, quantifiable financial gain resulting from working on a development goal).
- Time to complete development activity.
- Percent achievement of goal at key milestones toward deadline compared to planned progress level at those points.
- Number of development tools completed (number of training classes or rate of completion, number of self-directed development activities completed, and so forth).
- Employee's promotion resulting from a development activity.
- Results of pre- and post-development 360-degree assessment of the learner's skills and competencies.
- Improvement in employee's performance ratings metrics.
- Job title/grade of employee pre- and post-program.
- Percentage of completion of development activity.

Table 1-3 ▪ Matching Development Activities to Development Stage

STAGE		DESCRIPTION OF STAGE	PRIMARY DEVELOPMENT ACTIVITY
DISCOVERY	1 2 3	Awareness Acceptance Grasping the impact	Self-awareness assessment instruments Workshops Management counseling Counseling Therapy Services
DEVELOPMENT	4	Desire to improve	Management counseling
	5	Understanding (and articulating) the goal	Dialogues Projects Special assignments Tasks
	6	Capacity to work on self-improvement	Workshops Projects Special assignments Tasks On-the-job training Skill building
	7	Engaging in learning activities	Seminars Workshops Projects Special assignments Tasks On-the-job training Skill building Management counseling Counseling Therapy
DEMONSTRATION	8	Practicing the new competency	Projects Special assignments Tasks On-the-job training Skill building
	9	Seeking and accepting feedback and help	Workshops Projects Special assignments Tasks
	10	Demonstrating competence	Management coaching Management counseling On-the-job training

Source: Adapted from Drotter Human Resources, Inc.

_____

_____

_____

_____

Qualitative Measures

- Anecdotal evidence (via observation by others or self).
- Employee satisfaction and perception of development activity success/effectiveness at the beginning, middle, and end of the program.
- Participant pre- and post-program self-assessment to measure skills and competencies gained.
- Qualitative perception of participant effectiveness or satisfaction with the employee's work or style by peers, managers, clients, and others.
- Pre- and post-development activity completion.
- Written evaluations by participants pre- and post-program.

_____

_____

_____

_____

IMPLICATIONS, DEPENDENCIES, AND PREREQUISITES: OVERCOMING OBSTACLES

Successful people and organizations effectively plan for obstacles instead of getting blindsided by them. If you ask lots of questions about each goal, you can better anticipate potential obstacles and proactively incorporate their solutions into your goals. Each time you craft a goal, ask yourself:

- "What might be some dependencies that are attached to this goal?"
- "Are there any prerequisite conditions to reaching this goal?"
- "What are the potential barriers to achieving this goal? What potential obstacles might arise?"

- "What aspects of this goal's implications or dependencies are within the employee's control?"

- Be proactive.
- Anticipate obstacles.
- Plan your approach to overcome obstacles in your goals.
- Conquer obstacles preemptively—don't blame them passively.

For example, some goals depend on funding. Anticipate that funding will likely become an issue when you are setting the goal. Preemptively and proactively plan for how you will apply for and justify the funding and blend it into your plan to reach your desired outcome. Avoid the urge to keep your goals deliberately loose to accommodate any unexpected elements. While some obstacles may not be within your control, you can achieve better business results when you plan a strong, proactive approach.

DRAFTING YOUR GOALS

The next step is to define the development goal for the employee. Obtain a copy of your organization, department, and division goals and discuss with your employee how his development goals should align with the organizational goals. Use Table 1-4 to help the employee better understand how his job functions, roles, and responsibilities support your department's goals. The questions on the worksheet should help you write, and align, your SMART goals.

Competencies

The following sample of commonly used workplace competencies, and their definitions, can help you tailor your employee's development goals (Transportation Security Administration, n.d.). The list is not meant to be all-inclusive.

Accountability

Accountability means that effective controls are developed and maintained to ensure the integrity of the organization. Accountable people hold themselves and others accountable for rules and responsibilities and can be relied upon to ensure that projects within areas of specific responsibility are completed in a timely manner and

Table 1-4 ■ Goal Development Worksheet

Goal:
Department goal supported:
To support this goal, I will . . .
How do I measure success in reaching my goal? How do I quantify it?
What are my targets and/or milestones for the development period? (Specify dates.)
Does this goal meet the "SMART" criteria? Specific? Measurable? Aligned? Results-oriented? Time-bound?
Revised individual goal statement:

within budget. People who are accountable monitor and evaluate their plans, focus on results, and measure attainment of outcomes.

Conflict Management

Managing conflict involves identifying and taking steps to prevent potential situations that could result in unpleasant confrontations. Someone who is competent in this area manages and resolves conflicts and disagreements in a positive and constructive manner to minimize negative impact.

Creativity and Innovation

To be creative and innovative is to develop new insights into situations and apply new solutions to make organizational improvements.

When a work environment encourages creative thinking and innovation, it centers on designing and implementing new or cutting-edge programs/processes.

Cultural Awareness

Organizations that are culturally aware initiate and manage cultural change to have an impact on organizational effectiveness. Valuing cultural diversity and other individual differences in the workforce is key to being culturally aware, as is ensuring that the organization builds on cultural differences and that employees are treated in a fair and equitable manner.

Customer Service

Providing good customer service involves balancing the interests of a variety of clients and readily readjusting your priorities to respond to pressing and changing client demands. People who are competent in this area anticipate and meet the needs of clients, achieve quality end products, and are committed to continuous improvement of services.

Decisiveness

Decisive people exercise good judgment by making sound and well-informed decisions; perceive the impact and implications of decisions; make effective and timely decisions, even when data are limited or solutions produce unpleasant consequences; and are proactive and achievement oriented.

Financial Management

Successful financial managers demonstrate a broad understanding of financial management principles and have the marketing expertise necessary to ensure appropriate funding levels. They prepare, justify, and administer the budget for the program area, use cost-benefit thinking to set priorities, and monitor expenditures in support of programs and policies. Financial management also involves identifying cost-effective approaches, as well as procurement and contracting.

Flexibility

Being flexible means being open to change and new information. Flexible people adapt their behavior and work methods in response to new information, changing conditions, or unexpected obstacles, and they adjust rapidly to new situations warranting attention and resolution.

Influencing/Negotiating

Someone who persuades others, builds consensus through give and take, gains cooperation from others to obtain information and accomplish goals, and facilitates win-win situations is experienced at influencing/negotiating.

Interpersonal Skills

Individuals with good interpersonal skills consider and respond appropriately to the needs, feelings, and capabilities of different people in different situations; they are tactful, compassionate, and sensitive and treat others with respect.

Oral Communication

Making clear and convincing oral presentations to individuals or groups, listening effectively and clarifying information as needed, and facilitating an open exchange of ideas all describe successful oral communication.

Partnering

Partnering means developing networks and building alliances, engaging in cross-functional activities, collaborating across boundaries, and finding common ground with a widening range of stakeholders. Partners utilize their contacts to build and strengthen internal support bases.

Political Savvy

People with political savvy identify the internal and external politics that have an impact on the work of the organization. They approach each problem situation with a clear perception of organizational reality and recognize the impact of alternative courses of action.

Problem Solving

Problem solving involves identifying and analyzing problems, distinguishing between relevant and irrelevant information to make logical decisions, and providing solutions to individual and organizational problems.

Resilience

Resilient people deal effectively with pressure, maintain focus and intensity, and remain optimistic and persistent, even under adversity. They recover quickly from setbacks and effectively balance personal and work life.

Strategic Thinking

Strategic thinkers formulate effective strategies consistent with the business and competitive strategy of the organization in a global economy. They examine policy issues and strategic planning with a long-term perspective, determine objectives and set priorities, and anticipate potential threats or opportunities.

Team Building

Team building means inspiring, motivating, and guiding others toward goal accomplishments. Someone with this competency consistently develops and sustains cooperative working relationships; encourages and facilitates cooperation with the organization and with customer groups; fosters commitment, team spirit, pride, and trust; and develops leadership in others through coaching, mentoring, rewarding, and guiding employees.

Technology Management

Management of technology involves the use of efficient and cost-effective approaches to integrate technology into the workplace and improve program effectiveness. Technology managers develop strategies using new technology to enhance decision making and understand the impact of technological changes on the organization.

Written Communication

Written communication is the expression of facts and ideas in writing in a clear, convincing, and organized manner.

TRACKING AND MEASURING PROGRESS

One way to track progress on goals is to keep a journal. You can suggest that the employee use Table 1-5 to record goal progress or adapt it to fit her journaling style and goal needs as appropriate.

Table 1-5 ▪ Monthly Journal Template

Directions: Use this page (and additional pages as needed) to keep a monthly record of your development progress. You may journal or provide an answer for each specific topic.
Suggested Topics:
- Progress on goals and development.
- Possible opportunities or challenges to goals and development.
- Knowledge or skills gained in the development activity.
- Feedback received.
- Lessons learned (from both successes and challenges).
- Comments:

_____

_____

_____

_____

_____

_____

_____

_____

Source: Office of Human Resources (2011).

The employee should use Table 1-6 to prepare for her development. You can complete the worksheet together or ask the employee to create a first draft, after which you can review and provide suggestions and feedback. Finalize the plan together.

1. **Choose one to three developmental competencies.**
   Limit the number of developmental competencies

you work on at any given time so you can focus. You can always add more competencies to develop as you achieve your previous development goals. You might get ideas from your career goals, 360-degree feedback, or performance appraisals.

Table 1-6 ▪ Development Planning Worksheet

Development Competency #1	Development Goal (SMART):		
Development Activities	Resources and Support Needed	Timeline and Deadlines	Measures and Criteria for Success
Development Competency #2	Development Goal (SMART):		
Development Activities	Resources and Support Needed	Timeline and Deadlines	Measures and Criteria for Success
Development Competency #3	Development Goal (SMART):		
Development Activities	Resources and Support Needed	Timeline and Deadlines	Measures and Criteria for Success

2. **Define a developmental goal for each competency.** Develop a SMART goal that exactly describes your desired outcome.

3. **Identify development activities for each goal.** What specific activities will you need to complete in order to achieve each developmental goal? List them. Think of a mix between formal learning actions and informal, outside-the-classroom ones.

4. **List resources and support.** Determine the support and resources that you will need to implement the developmental activities. They include peers and leaders, time, money, and materials.

5. **Define timelines, milestones, and deadlines.** Select the final deadline for completing each developmental activity as well as any interim milestones. It is a good idea to also set an overall deadline for the achievement of each developmental goal.

6. **Determine measures and success criteria.** How will you measure success? List these criteria.

To help you get a better idea of how to complete the development planning worksheet, Table 1-7 provides a sample completed development plan.

MAKING YOUR BUSINESS CASE

As an employee developer, you understand why the development method you have chosen is a great idea. However, your leadership or other potential sponsors, advocates, and supporters need to buy into it as well. Use Table 1-8 to plan your strategy for convincing key stakeholders to get on board with this development method. Use a separate sheet for every potential development method you want to promote.

- Development method:

  _____

- Employee to use it (optional):

  _____

Table 1-7 ▪ Sample Development Worksheet

Development Competency: Flexibility	Development Goal (SMART): Toby quickly adapts his behavior and work methods in response to new information, changing conditions, or unexpected obstacles. He adjusts rapidly to new situations warranting attention and resolution.		
Development Activities	Resources and Support Needed	Timeline and Deadlines	Measures and Criteria for Success
Toby will read at least three books on change and flexibility and write a summary of the key lessons he can apply from each book.	Identify and purchase first book or borrow from library. Repeat for second and third books. Manager will be available to meet with Toby for each report for one hour.	Obtain first book by Friday of next week. Read first book and write report by the end of the month. Discuss with manager by first Friday of next month. Repeat for second and third book. Complete all three books by end of second quarter.	Toby has read and reported on at least three books about change and flexibility by the end of second quarter.
Toby will take on a more observant, quiet role during problem solving and project planning meetings to allow and understand multiple views and perspectives for each problem. He will also personally write three alternative explanations to each idea or judgment that he thinks of before articulating his opinion in meetings.	Journal or record-keeping notebook or electronic document for insights and generating alternatives. Inform staff members about this challenge and develop a special hand signal they could give him if Toby becomes active when multiple other views have not yet been expressed.	Begin immediately and conduct this behavior during every staff or management meeting where a deliberation of a problem and possible solutions occurs. Journal as soon as possible after a meeting to reflect and capture insights and lessons learned. Check in with manager to report progress and insights once every two weeks for the first two months, less frequently after (based on mutual agreement at that time).	Toby will have regular journal records of attempts showing increasingly more observant and less active behavior during deliberations. By the end of the second quarter, Toby will have an 85 percent success rate of withholding his ideas and comments from deliberations until at least ¾ of those present have actively participated with their ideas, as reported by him in his reflection journals.

Table 1-7 ▪ Sample Development Worksheet (Continued)

Development Competency: Flexibility	**Development Goal (SMART):** Toby quickly adapts his behavior and work methods in response to new information, changing conditions, or unexpected obstacles. He adjusts rapidly to new situations warranting attention and resolution.		
Development Activities	Resources and Support Needed	Timeline and Deadlines	Measures and Criteria for Success
Toby will complete a job rotation assignment in a department/location that is known to be under a lot of stress and pressure to gain a new perspective on organizational issues and develop new ways of working, especially in a challenging environment. He will keep a journal of his challenges and insights and debrief his manager afterward to identify what was most challenging or difficult for him and how he could handle those aspects more effectively.	Identify location for job rotation. Correspond with rotation manager and ensure availability of rotation assignment. Determine a succession plan for Toby's current role for the duration of the rotation. Communicate plan to staff and management and gain their support.	List 5–8 possible assignment ideas by end of month. Finalize the target assignment location by end of second quarter. Identify succession plan by end of second quarter. Communicate plan to staff and management by mid-July. Begin rotation by end of August. End rotation by the next January. Conduct debrief discussion within two weeks from return to current role.	Toby will have successfully planned for and completed a six-month rotational assignment with a focus on developing flexibility under pressure and new perspectives for organizational issues by year's end.

Table 1-8 ▪ Preparation Worksheet

Stakeholder	Predisposition: Pro, Con, or Neutral?	What Do They Care About/ Hot Buttons?	Possible Selling Points/ Benefits That Will Motivate Them	Possible Objections and My Response

As you and your employee prepare to work on the development plan, use the checklist in Table 1-9 to ensure you don't forget any key action items.

Table 1-9 ▪ Predevelopment Planning Worksheet

Pre-_____ [Development Method] **Preparation Checklist**
• Define the desired outcomes for this activity or program.
• Design measure(s) to assess the activity or program's progress and success.
• Define ways to ensure that employee time and effort are well spent and purposeful.
• Develop a communication plan to clarify the purpose and desired outcomes of this initiative/ activity to the appropriate stakeholders to gain support.
• Create a plan to protect the time from interruptions (if appropriate).
• Identify and obtain the necessary supplies and resources.
• Establish appropriate coverage to support ongoing customer service or business processes and operations while working on development tasks.
• Identify record-keeping and reporting mechanisms to maintain an account of the learner's progress and accomplishments.
• Plan ways to celebrate progress and goal achievement.

IMPLEMENTATION

Use Table 1-10 to think through some of your ideas for each development method.

1. What are some possible opportunities for the employee to try this method of development?
2. What would be the learning objectives for each of these learning opportunities? What are the goals for the

Table 1-10 ▪ Implementation Planning Worksheet

Learning Opportunities	Learning Objective	Time Required	Resources Required	Supports/ Advocates?	Other Considerations?

employee's learning and development if she engages in this learning task?

3. How long will the employee need to work on this learning task (estimate)? What might be logical time increments if she can't work on it all at once (if appropriate)?

4. What resources will the employee need to have for each learning task (for example, supplies, information, equipment, or space)?

5. Whose support will this task require? Who can the employee recruit to cheer her on and help protect her time while she works on it?

6. What are other considerations, possible obstacles, or contingencies you must identify to ensure success?

Transferring Learning Back to the Job

The true benefit of learning is results that positively affect the employee's day-to-day job. For each development method, ask these questions:

- What did the employee learn?
- What new knowledge did the employee gain?
- What new skills did the employee develop?
- Can the employee quantify these results?

- How does the employee track his success?
- How does the employee tout his success?

Results and Benefits

For each development assignment, clearly articulate the learning results and translate them to personal and organizational benefits for the employee and the organization. This practice helps solidify the business case for spending time and resources on development. Use Table 1-11 to help you.

Table 1-11 ▪ Results and Benefits Analysis Worksheet

Results/Skills Developed	Benefit
• _____	• _____
• _____	• _____
• _____	• _____
• _____	• _____
• _____	• _____
• _____	• _____
• _____	• _____
• _____	• _____
• _____	• _____
• _____	• _____
• _____	• _____

RESOURCES

Brown, T. (2010, April). Having Their Backs: Improving Managers' Skills in Developing Others. *T+D*. Available from http://store.astd.org/Default.aspx?tabid=167&ProductId=21108

Grote, D. (2002). *The Performance Appraisal Question and Answer Book.* New York: AMACOM.

Ivanoff, P., and S.J. Drotter. (2008). *Coaching and Mentoring for Achieving BNL Strategy: A Self-Help Workbook.* Brookhaven National Laboratory. Drotter Human Resources, Inc. Available from http://training.bnl.gov/course/SupNews/LPinfo/CMWorkbook.doc

Latham, G.P. (2009, July). Motivating Employee Performance Through Goal Setting. In *Handbook of Principles of Organizational Behavior: Indispensable Knowledge for Evidence-Based Management*, 2nd edition, ed. E.A. Locke. Chichester, UK: John Wiley and Sons.

Office of Disaster Assistance. (2010, March 17). *Guidebook: Individual Development Planning: General Guidelines for Employees and Managers.* U.S. Small Business Administration. Retrieved from http://www.opm.gov/WIKI/uploads/docs/Wiki/OPM/training/SBA%20IDP%20Guidebook.pdf

Office of Human Resources. (2011, August 16). *NIH-HHS Mentoring Program: Activities for Mentor/Mentee Pairs. National Institutes of Health*, U.S. Department of Health and Human Services. Retrieved from http://trainingcenter.nih.gov/hhs_mentoring.html#competencies

Transportation Security Administration. (n.d.). *Competency Development.* U.S. Department of Homeland Security. Retrieved from http://www.tsa.gov/join/benefits/competencies.shtm

Chapter 2

SOLO FLYER: SELF-DIRECTED LEARNING

WHAT IS IT?

Self-directed learning is a broad type of employee development. In a way, we could probably lump (almost) every other chapter in this book under this umbrella. The distinction to draw, as far as this book is concerned, is that this type of learning is completed individually, by the employee, with little to no support from any external organizational structures or other people. Self-directed learning is self-powered, self-administered, and self-motivated learning.

While it could take a multitude of forms, the most common types of self-directed learning are reading, listening to prerecorded information, watching videotaped information, and following printed or recorded instructions to complete a task. In other words, the learning may be visual, auditory, or kinesthetic and performed by readers, observers, listeners, or doers independently on their own time and at their own pace.

Reading

Visual learners learn best by reading or looking at graphic representations of information. Much of the self-directed learning that we typically experience is done in this manner: reading books, articles, newsletters, websites, blogs, charts, graphs, graphic models, and any other written or graphic depiction of information. Learners can learn visually from printed or online material anywhere because it is easily accessible and transportable. Self-directed learners can read in a library, at home, or in the office, or even hang out at a bookstore and skim all the books that interest them in a particular section. They can read online on their computer at their desk, on their laptop at a café, on their e-reader on the beach, on their iPad at the park, or on their mobile device at the airport.

Listening

Auditory learners learn best by listening to audio delivery of information. Self-directed auditory learning involves listening to recorded information in the form of audiobooks, recorded lectures or presentations, or any other recording of audio information. This type of learning can also take place anywhere because it can be done via the computer or laptop, using the built-in speakers or plugged-in headphones. It can also be performed via the many different kinds of audio devices available, such as iPads, MP3 players, and mobile devices. Learners can learn in most places where reading would also be possible, and in places where reading would not work so well, such as while driving, riding a bike, or jogging. EMC supplements its executives' training by providing participating learners with preloaded iPods featuring playlists of executive summaries of leading business books, for example.

Watching

A form of learning that combines audio and visual learning, watching recorded audiovisual information is a highly engaging way to learn, especially if the information is presented in an interesting and attention-grabbing way. Learners can use a computer, VCR, or DVD player at home, in the office, or anywhere with a portable player or a laptop, an iPad, or even a smartphone. With the explosion of video-sharing services such as YouTube, the amount of recorded audiovisual information that can be instructional has grown exponentially. Recordings can vary from mini-tutorials by pedestrian peers via YouTube, to videos of world-renowned experts on TED.org, to National Geographic specials with multimillion-dollar recording budgets. Additional ways of audiovisual learning include visiting cultural institutions that use headsets and prerecorded tours, such as museums, zoos, and arboretums.

Doing

Tactile or kinesthetic learning is learning by doing. Some learners learn best not by reading, listening, or watching someone explain how to do something, but by trying to do it themselves. It is learning through the body, through movement and the sense of touch. Self-directed kinesthetic learning involves either learning by trial and error, organically, or learning by following written, auditory, or audiovisual recordings. Depending on the subject matter, kinesthetic learning may or may not need any special settings or materials. If learners are trying to learn how to cook a Catalan-style Spanish stew, they need ingredients, utensils, and kitchen appliances. But if they are trying to learn how to create a spreadsheet in Microsoft Excel, they need a computer or laptop with the Excel program, but no special location or any other tools. This type of learning can also include shadowing, observing, and practicing skills of role models in the work environment or in specialized locations such as factories, workshops, stores, and other institutions.

WHO SHOULD TRY IT?

Learners are empowered to set goals and achieve learning objectives that are totally customized to their learning levels and needs. Self-directed learning encourages responsibility and ownership, and puts learners in control of their learning. Therefore, to fully benefit, learners must be self-motivated and independent. Any learner, at any level, in any part of the organization, can benefit from self-directed learning because it can be tailored to suit one's individual learning level. And, in fact, we can estimate that just about every employee engages in some kind of self-directed learning every year.

Learners who are not self-motivated, or who have significant concerns or inhibitions about the subject matter or their ability to be successful, would probably not find this kind of learning appealing. They may not be able to successfully navigate the lessons independent of external reinforcement, modeling, or accountability structures. Sometimes learners are not interested in learning something, because they don't value the learning goals, don't agree with the purpose, or are unwilling to perform the learning tasks. These types of unwilling participants would find it difficult to complete self-directed learning as their chief form of development.

In order to determine if learners are ready and well suited for self-directed learning, ask them to complete the self-assessment in Figure 2-1.

HOW DOES IT BENEFIT THE LEARNER?

Self-directed learning can benefit learners who engage in these activities in several ways. Self-directed learning:

- Allows the learners to drive the learning method and process.
- Builds independence.
- Provides total freedom in implementing the chosen learning strategy.
- Allows the learners to learn according to their preferred learning style.
- Permits flexibility in most cases to begin learning at the learners' current level rather than at some generic set point.
- Helps the learners develop skills in setting goals, identifying options, and evaluating outcomes.
- Allows the learners almost unlimited opportunities to learn new information and skills because it is completed for little to no cost and can be done almost anywhere, anytime.

Figure 2.1 ▪ Self-Directed Learning Readiness

Respond to the statements by placing an X along each spectrum.

1. I love to learn.

| Not very true of me | Somewhat true of me | Very much true of me |

2. If I want to learn something, I figure out how to learn it.

| Not very true of me | Somewhat true of me | Very much true of me |

3. Learning is a lifelong pursuit.

| Not very true of me | Somewhat true of me | Very much true of me |

4. When I'm interested in something, I don't mind working hard to get it done.

| Not very true of me | Somewhat true of me | Very much true of me |

5. I know what I want to learn.

| Not very true of me | Somewhat true of me | Very much true of me |

6. If I don't understand something, I try to learn more about it.

| Not very true of me | Somewhat true of me | Very much true of me |

7. Getting started on new projects is easy for me.

| Not very true of me | Somewhat true of me | Very much true of me |

8. If there is information that I need but don't have, I know where to get it.

| Not very true of me | Somewhat true of me | Very much true of me |

9. I like to be involved in deciding what will be learned and how when I'm in a learning experience.

| Not very true of me | Somewhat true of me | Very much true of me |

10. I'm the only one truly responsible for my own development.

| Not very true of me | Somewhat true of me | Very much true of me |

11. I can learn things on my own better than most people.

| Not very true of me | Somewhat true of me | Very much true of me |

12. I'm good at working on my own.

| Not very true of me | Somewhat true of me | Very much true of me |

13. I wish there were more time available for learning because I have many things I would like to learn.

| Not very true of me | Somewhat true of me | Very much true of me |

14. If there is something I have decided to learn, I can find time for it, no matter how busy I am.

| Not very true of me | Somewhat true of me | Very much true of me |

Source: Guglielmino (1977).

HOW DOES IT BENEFIT THE ORGANIZATION?

Self-directed learning benefits not only the learners but also the organization because it:

- Allows the organization more opportunities to be flexible toward its learners because not all people learn the same way.
- Focuses on outcomes while allowing employees to choose how those skills are acquired.
- Provides limitless development opportunities for independent, self-motivated employees.
- Encourages personal responsibility and ownership.
- Is often more cost-effective than other development methods.
- Helps the organization to provide equal development opportunities to employees across all levels and areas of the business.

WHAT COMPETENCIES AND SKILLS CAN IT DEVELOP?

The competencies that can be developed through self-directed learning are virtually unlimited. Because it is so multifaceted and can be performed by anyone in almost any place, learning independently can really be successfully achieved in almost any realm. Here are a few examples of competencies that may be developed with self-directed learning:

- Accountability—by working independently on their development goals in this way, employees can definitely develop their ability to hold themselves accountable to agreed-upon plans and responsibilities and ensure that the goals are achieved in a timely manner and within budget.
- Conflict management—as an example of a specific topic of interest for self-directed learning, employees who want to develop their ability to manage and resolve conflicts in a positive and constructive manner could work on learning these skills in a self-directed way.

- Problem solving—both in selecting the media for the learning activity and in the focus of the subject matter, employees who want to improve their ability to identify and analyze problems and provide logical solutions could do so in a self-directed way.

HOW DOES IT WORK?

How to Prepare

Learners and their supervisors or developers must decide and contract upon the answers to these preparation questions:

- What are the desired outcomes for this self-directed learning activity?
- What measures will be used to assess learners' progress and success?
- How will learners' dedicated learning time be protected from disruptions?
- What supplies are needed? What other resources are required? Who needs to be involved?
- How will learners record and report an account of their progress and learning as well as their accomplishments?
- How will you celebrate learners' progress and goal achievement?

Ways to Track Progress and Results

Tracking progress on self-directed learning will follow varied methods depending on how the learning itself is taking place. Here are some ideas to get you started:

- Compare the number of pages read, or minutes listened or watched, to the total number of pages or minutes in the selected item.
- Compare the number of selected books, articles, recordings, podcasts, or videos to the number actually completed.
- Answer comprehension questions about the concepts, vocabulary, and other information that learners should have learned by reading, listening, or watching.

- Measure the learner's ability to perform and skillfulness in performing tasks that were described in the material she read, listened to, or watched.
- Other ideas:

_____

_____

_____

_____

_____

_____

Implementation Tips

Match learner motivation and level of self-directedness to the learning goals and methods selected. Learners who are self-motivated to achieve the learning goals and who self-direct and agree with the learning methods are much more likely to enjoy the learning approach and successfully complete the self-directed learning tasks.

Create a formal learning contract or list explicit goals and expectations. While all learners may learn on their own in an informal way, in order to fully benefit from the outcomes (both for the learner and for the organization), you must formalize the approach and show that it is not an afterthought or a cop-out, but rather an intentional learning method with specific goals that will be measured.

Track progress and follow up with the learner periodically as agreed upon at the onset of the learning program. Just as it is important to show seriousness when setting the initial intentions and goals, it is crucial to follow through on those plans and follow up with the learner to show that the organization takes this learning just as seriously and expects just as much success as with formal learning events. If you appear to have forgotten about this learning, it will have a strong chance to become forgotten or dismissed by the learner as well.

Provide opportunities for self-directed learners to reflect on what they are learning. One of the ways this will naturally happen is during your goal-tracking and milestone measurement efforts.

Recognize and reward learners when they have met their learning objectives. Remember the adage, "out of sight, out of mind"? Because this type of learning does not happen right in front of others who can support the learners as they overcome hurdles or achieve success with their goals, you will have to make a conscious effort to positively recognize success, both intermediary and final, toward goal accomplishment. What gets celebrated gets repeated.

Promote learning networks, study circles, and learning exchanges. Even though self-directed learning can and does happen in isolation, it doesn't have to be that way. Often, self-directed learners benefit from the sense of support and camaraderie that they get from belonging to a community of learners.

Required Resources and Supports

Learning materials—take advantage of books, articles, recordings, videos, simulation models, and other learning materials based on the type of learning approach selected.

Learning space and equipment—does the learner need to be in a quiet environment to more successfully concentrate on the learning? Consider this requirement and be prepared to provide a space that is conducive to the kind of learning that will be performed. If reading, ensure that the location is quiet and has sufficient light as well as a comfortable chair. If listening, provide headphones if learners are planning to listen in their normal work environment or in any space shared with others so as to reduce disruptions to colleagues. This suggestion also applies to watching videos. Also ensure that the audio and video player is in good repair and that there is sufficient bandwidth if listening or watching over an Internet connection. If the learning requires hands-on manipulation of models or materials, ensure that the space allows for successful accomplishment of the practice and that safety precautions have been implemented, as appropriate.

Supervisor and peer support—get learners' supervisors on board with the idea of developing skills via self-directed learning. The supervisors will champion the learners' cause and support them with time and other resources. If the learners' peers (co-workers) are recruited to support them, they may be able to help the learners with resources, with materials, and by protecting them from unneeded disruptions so they can successfully engage in quiet, focused learning.

Concerns/Downsides

Some opponents of this kind of development activity have voiced these concerns:

Concern: Motivation. Self-directed learning can seem like a great idea at first, but learners' motivation and commitment to completing the learning task might begin to wane with time. Also, when approaching the learning on their own, learners may not have sufficient motivation to overcome obstacles such as difficulty with comprehension or competing priorities interfering with the learning schedule.

Overcome it: The best candidates for self-directed learning are employees with initiative and a self-propelled drive to learn, because they have better odds for sustaining motivation in the face of competing priorities or obstacles. Therefore, one of the best ways to avoid this problem is to ensure that you select the right candidates for this type of development. That said, motivation can wane even for the most self-driven learner when there is no support, no external performance expectations, or no consequences for failure. So the second most important protector of motivation is external support from the supervisor. That means providing sufficient resources, planning goals and milestones, following up on progress, measuring goal accomplishment, and celebrating success.

Concern: Time. Won't self-directed learning require learners to spend a lot of time away from their job duties? And how can learners protect their time from being ferreted away by other work priorities when there is no formal learning event with a start and end time or other people joining in?

Overcome it: First, self-directed learning doesn't necessarily require a lot of time. Learners can decide in advance, with their supervisors, how much time they can afford to spend on learning and what learning materials may fit in that allotted time-frame. If they can only afford to spend one hour per week in self-directed learning mode, learners should not select an entire two-hour video to watch at once. However, they can watch it in two separate one-hour installments over the course of two weeks. If learners don't carefully guard their planned time for learning, there is a danger that it will get cut into or dissipate without much fanfare. It will be important to think of possible obstacles in advance and plan strategies to overcome them. Some ideas include physically leaving their workspace and moving to a secluded, private location for the duration of the learning so they don't get pulled into disruptions from email, phone calls, or co-workers. They could also ask their supervisors and colleagues to help them protect their designated learning time by sharing their goals and intentions with them and asking for their active support. Just as the learning is self-directed, so must the protection of the learning be self-initiated and self-implemented.

Concern: Feeling neglected/low value perception. Some people might feel that having to engage in such a low-cost, low-visibility learning method means that their supervisor and organization don't value their development enough. They might see this as cop-out development or as a message that they don't merit a more formal learning program and are being relegated to a "leftover" or "afterthought" learning approach.

Overcome it: Perception is a powerful force, and it should not be ignored. The supervisor and organization should carefully plan to communicate the value of self-directed learning and of the learners to the organization up front. The more this learning approach is preemptively described in a positive way, the less chance there is that employees will arrive at those erroneous conclusions about the intentions of the supervisor or organization. Authentically and transparently explain why this method is selected, framing it as a win–win value proposition. Also, remind employees of other valuable learning opportunities that are available, or were in the recent past, to ensure that they don't forget the rest of the picture when it comes to their development options.

RESOURCES

Candy, P.C. (1991). *Self-Direction for Lifelong Learning: A Comprehensive Guide to Theory and Practice.* San Francisco: Jossey-Bass.

Government of Alberta, Human Resources and Employment. (2005). *Skills by Design: Strategies for Employee Development.* Retrieved from http://alis.alberta.ca/pdf/cshop/SkillsDesign.pdf

Guglielmino, L.M. (n.d.). *What Is the Self-Directed Learning Readiness Scale?* Retrieved from http://www.lpasdlrs.com/

Knowles, M.S. (1975). *Self-Directed Learning: A Guide for Learners and Teachers.* Englewood Cliffs, NJ: Prentice Hall/Cambridge.

Lowry, C.M. (2003). *Supporting and Facilitating Self-Directed Learning.* National Teaching and Learning Foundation. Retrieved from http://www.ntlf.com/html/lib/bib/89dig.htm

Smith, M.K. (2002). Malcolm Knowles, Informal Adult Education, Self-Direction and Andragogy. *The Encyclopedia of Informal Education.* Retrieved from www.infed.org/thinkers/et-knowl.htm

Sontakey, A. (2009). Compress Your Learning Curve: Improve Enterprise Learning Through Collaboration and Knowledge Sharing. *Infosys SET-Labs Briefings 7*(3). Retrieved from http://www.infosys.com/infosys-labs/publications/setlabs-briefings/Pages/compress-your-learning-curve.aspx

Chapter 3

DOING GOOD: LEARNING BY VOLUNTEERING

WHAT IS IT?

Volunteering involves providing your knowledge, skills, and abilities, as well as your time and energy, without establishing an employment relationship and usually without any monetary compensation. Employees who take on volunteer roles are able to build new skills and practice existing skills in a different setting from their day-to-day jobs. They can try something that is different from their usual work and bring back those skills, thereby adding value to their employer by improving their current job performance. They may even enhance the succession management efforts of their employers because they become ready to move into positions of greater responsibility faster and more effectively than they would had they not taken on the volunteer role. The best part about this employee development strategy is it doesn't cost the organization nearly as much as sending the employee to costly training workshops or hiring a coach. In fact, it often costs the organization nothing.

For example, according to the report "Global Companies Volunteering Globally," produced by the Global Corporate Volunteer Council (GCVC) of the International Association for Volunteer Effort (IAVE), Timberland supports service projects led by employees who learn new skills and gain valuable project management and leadership experience that develops them professionally. The company sees these projects as positively contributing to the brand and to the business. Another example cited is Samsung, a company that values employees who communicate effectively with various communities. Samsung encourages employees to volunteer with nongovernmental organizations (NGOs) to complement Samsung's in-house training programs geared to enhance professional competencies such as negotiation and communication with external audiences (Realized Worth, 2011a, 2011b).

While there are many ways to volunteer, let's focus on three main categories of volunteering as employee development methods: job-related volunteering, context-changing volunteering, and teaching or mentoring volunteering.

Job-Related Volunteering

One way to enhance your employees' skills and knowledge in their current professions is to find a volunteer opportunity in the same type of job role and industry. For example, if employees specialize in accounting, they could find a volunteer job that involves being the treasurer of a local nonprofit. Or if employees are in public relations, they could volunteer as the PR coordinator for their trade association's local chapter or for a local animal rescue organization. The volunteer job would be related to their paid job.

Context-Changing Volunteering

Another way for employees to gain new skills and knowledge is to find a volunteer role that lets them experience a whole new industry, try a different field, or take on tasks that are in a different kind of role than the ones they perform daily in their paid jobs. For example, if employees are professionally in the field of accounting, they might take on a volunteer role that requires writing marketing collateral for their professional association (same field, different role). Or perhaps they could try their hand at being the president of the board of directors of their local soup kitchen (different field, different role). Or they could take a volunteer job reading newspaper articles to elderly residents at an assisted-living facility (different industry, different role).

Teaching or Mentoring Volunteering

A third key way to learn in a volunteer capacity is to become a teacher or a mentor of some type. There are lots of different ways and places you could do this. For example, you could volunteer to teach Sunday school lessons (or their equivalent) at your place of worship. You could volunteer to become a mentor to a person who is just entering your profession. Or you might choose to lead training seminars or webinars for your professional association on a subject with which you are familiar or one that you would like to learn about.

> By *learning you will teach;*
> by *teaching you will understand.*
> —Latin Proverb

"There is no question that volunteering is an outstanding professional development tool because of the real experience it provides," says James H. Quigley, CEO of Deloitte & Touche USA LLP (HR .BLR.com, 2005).

WHO SHOULD TRY IT?

Everyone should try this way to develop new skills and knowledge! Why is it for everyone? Because it is totally customizable to individual employees' development needs and can be crafted to match specific parameters such as their current work situations, availability, and future plans. And, because this method can be used for developing any type of knowledge or skill, it is applicable to all fields, industries, development levels, and job types.

One of the things that is unique about volunteering as an employee development method is that it doesn't really cost anything (except for time and effort), and it can be done in tandem with employees' current jobs because most volunteer roles are performed during off-work hours. It gives employees a chance to do the types of activities they would love to do at work but simply don't get the opportunity to do—either because they are not yet seen as "ready" to perform them in their jobs or because there isn't yet an opportunity or a need there. As volunteers, they often get to "try on" roles, work, and experiences that their paid jobs cannot or will not let them try.

Help your employees assess their readiness for a volunteer development opportunity using the self-assessment in Figure 3-1.

Figure 3-1 ▪ Self-Assessment: Volunteering Readiness

Respond to the statements by placing an X along each spectrum.

1. I enjoy venturing to new and unfamiliar places.

Not very true of me · Somewhat true of me · Very much true of me

2. I like being in an unfamiliar setting where I am outside my comfort zone because I always learn something new that way.

Not very true of me · Somewhat true of me · Very much true of me

3. I want to increase my network within my professional community.

Not very true of me · Somewhat true of me · Very much true of me

4. I want to increase my influence within my professional community.

Not very true of me · Somewhat true of me · Very much true of me

5. I would enjoy contributing my skills to a community organization whose mission I support.

Not very true of me · Somewhat true of me · Very much true of me

6. I would enjoy developing new skills I've been interested in learning but that my job doesn't allow me the opportunity to try.

Not very true of me · Somewhat true of me · Very much true of me

7. I would like to take on a higher-responsibility leadership role.

Not very true of me · Somewhat true of me · Very much true of me

8. I would like to mentor or teach others.

Not very true of me · Somewhat true of me · Very much true of me

9. I would like to "give back" by leveraging my knowledge and skills.

Not very true of me · Somewhat true of me · Very much true of me

HOW DOES IT BENEFIT THE LEARNER?

Employees who volunteer receive a number of benefits. Volunteering allows employees to:

- Enhance job-relevant skills while making a contribution to communities.
- Gain a fresh perspective on old problems and issues.
- See the world through a different lens to open new avenues of creative problem solving.
- Increase cultural awareness.
- Solve problems.
- Reduce complacency and boredom of routine.
- Think in new and more creative ways in their current roles.
- Increase job satisfaction.
- Become more engaged in their work.
- Experience job enrichment.
- Find new and increased awareness of personal strengths, competencies, values, management and learning styles, and areas for development.
- Develop their careers (an employee who volunteers accumulates experience more quickly than an employee who does not volunteer).
- Increase their network of contacts outside the organization.

HOW DOES IT BENEFIT THE ORGANIZATION?

There are also benefits to the organization when its employees volunteer. Volunteering:

- Complements an organization's formal online, classroom, and on-the-job training programs.
- Provides employees with reality-based experiential learning rather than that simulated in a classroom or online.
- Allows employees to develop in a supportive environment (often the performance expectations of recipients of volunteer services are more forgiving than those of recipients of commercial-based services).

43

- Provides greater opportunity to develop employees' skills earlier in their careers, generating greater speed to competence and improving succession management and leadership bench strength.
- Accelerates skill development for key employees.
- Enhances the leadership pipeline, building leadership bench strength.
- Increases goodwill with employees, clients, and the public.
- Brands the organization as an "employer of choice," especially among Generation Y/Millennials who say they want work with a sense of purpose and community (Wojcik, 2008).
- Improves partnering opportunities with community organizations.
- Increases employee loyalty.
- Enhances employee engagement.
- Improves recruiting capabilities.
- Increases retention of experienced employees.
- Expands problem-solving resources.
- Provides a healthy work-life balance.
- Boosts enthusiasm and productivity.
- Improves talent management capacity during a recession.

WHAT COMPETENCIES AND SKILLS CAN IT DEVELOP?

This development method is totally customizable and therefore can fit any kind of development need. If employees are looking to develop their leadership skills, they can take volunteer leadership roles. If employees want to develop their marketing and copywriting skills, then volunteering in a marketing capacity is for them. If employees want to develop financial management skills, they can find volunteer jobs that let them run the budget and financial records for a nonprofit organization in their communities.

A 2004 study of employees who volunteered as part of a program offered by their employer, Barclays Bank in England, reported that more than 60 percent of the volunteers' managers saw improvements in their staff's communication skills, and 56 percent reported increases in their staff's leadership skills as a result of volunteering. This study also showed that skills tended to increase with the frequency of volunteering. The more times the employees volunteered, the more they reported that their skills (such as decision-making) increased (Institute for Volunteering Research, 2004).

In the Deloitte Volunteer IMPACT Survey, 86 percent of employed Americans said volunteering can have a positive impact on their careers. The skills they specifically improved as a result of volunteering were decision-making (88 percent), negotiating (82 percent), problem solving (89 percent), and leadership (93 percent; HR.BLR.com, 2005).

HOW DOES IT WORK?

How to Prepare

Consider these preparation questions before embarking on volunteer opportunities:

- What are the desired outcomes for employees as a result of engaging in this volunteer work?
- What measures will be used to assess their progress and success?
- What might you or your organization need to do to ensure that this kind of investment of the employees' time and effort is well spent?
- What supplies are needed? What other resources are required?
- How will the employees record and report an account of their progress and learning as well as their accomplishments?
- How will they celebrate progress and goal achievement?

Then consider the following steps for preparation:

1. Research available volunteering opportunities. Contact the local chapter of your professional association for leads on opportunities in your industry or field. Contact the

local office of other organizations that interest you. Talk to friends, colleagues, and family about what you want to do, and ask for referrals. Look in local publications and on community websites to identify possible opportunities.

2. Contact volunteer organizations to learn more about various options, the required experience level, and what commitment is needed.

3. Identify the steps required for the recruitment and onboarding process with your chosen volunteer organization. Some organizations have a more formal recruiting process, while others are quite informal about it. Take the cue from them and find out what they prefer. If needed, send your résumé and any other required materials to the volunteer organization and arrange for an interview or a meeting to discuss next steps.

4. Develop talking points to discuss with your supervisor— what skills, competencies, or knowledge will you be able to develop through engaging in this volunteer opportunity? How will the new skills, competencies, or knowledge support your current and future performance in your job? Think of the benefits to the employer, not to you, as you make your case.

5. Schedule and conduct a meeting with your employer to discuss your intentions and solidify a development plan. Your goal is to garner your employer's support. Remember, you can still volunteer even if you don't succeed with this step, but having support is always easier and smoother than going it alone.

6. Plan your schedule and dedicate the time that your new volunteer role will require you to invest. Rearrange or renegotiate previous commitments as necessary.

Ways to Track Progress and Results

Measures and tracking methods differ for different development goals.

- Employees working on developing financial management skills can track the organization's financial success and the accuracy of the financial records as measures of the results of their improved skills.
- If employees are working to develop leadership or influencing skills, they can survey the satisfaction of their constituents in the volunteer organization with their performance. Journaling will also be helpful to reflect on experiences and lessons learned and to notice progress.
- Other ideas:

_____

_____

_____

_____

_____

_____

Implementation Tips

Supervisor support helps, but isn't a requirement. The more supportive an employee's work environment is of volunteering, the better. However, many volunteers do the work on their own, on the side, even if unsupported, since it should not interfere with their ability to fully perform their paid job duties.

Focus on purpose. Sometimes organizations worry that the volunteer role will grow too much or take too much time or energy. This can happen especially easily if employees are not focused singularly on what they are seeking to accomplish. The more laser-like their focus is on their goals and purpose, the better they will be able to say no to work that does not help achieve those. Employees will have to guard themselves from becoming stretched thin or burned out. Everyone wants to help more and do more, but the truth is we only have a finite number of hours and amount of energy available, so we have to use them wisely.

Track insights and learning. Employees should use tools such as journaling to reflect on their experiences, insights, and lessons learned. It is easier to realize how the volunteering role is making a difference on their competency if they reflect regularly, notice, and note.

There's more to it than skill building. Volunteering is giving freely of our time, energy, and skills. Here, we are viewing it through the lens of employee development, but often there are other benefits employees can gain from volunteering. Some of the most common benefits are the opportunity to make a difference in the community, a chance to "give back" or "pay it forward" by helping others, increasing our professional and personal network of contacts, gaining insider information about opportunities, and developing a sense of camaraderie with our fellow volunteers and the people we serve through our volunteer roles.

Know when to quit. There will come a time when employees feel like they have learned all they can from the volunteer role, or that the benefits no longer outweigh the costs of spending time in this pursuit. It is key that employee volunteers don't overextend themselves and prolong their volunteer roles past that usefulness and satisfaction. Often, their performance will start to slip, they will begin to resent the time and energy volunteering requires, and they will no longer derive the pleasure of doing the work. Employee volunteers should find a responsible and efficient way to exit their volunteer roles when it's that time, or identify another role or responsibility in the same organization that can correct the imbalance and allow them to continue to develop and be gratified.

Required Resources and Supports

If contacts and information exist about possible volunteer opportunities, share them with the learner.

Supervisor and peer support—get learners' supervisors onboard with the idea of developing skills by volunteering. Once the supervisors buy into the idea, they will champion the learners' cause and support them with time and other resources. The learners' co-workers or staff also must be encouraged to support them and understand their goals, if possible.

Concerns/Downsides

Some of the opponents of this kind of development activity have voiced these concerns:

Concern: Not enough time. Employees feel that they don't have time to volunteer—they're too busy with their paid jobs and other life responsibilities.

Overcome it: First, we make time for what is important. If employees really want to develop new skills, competencies, or knowledge, they will find the time for it. In addition, the great thing about volunteering is that employees can find a role (or invent one) that fits within their particular time constraints. Unlike a paid job where there are a set number of hours that are required or there is a set amount of work a person must produce, often organizations that rely on volunteer fuel recognize the need to tailor the job to the person's ability and availability. They will usually be happy to accommodate the volunteers and take what they can give because it's better than nothing. When you don't have to pay salaries, there is no limit to the number of people you can recruit—even if each of them only works 10 hours a month.

Concern: Lack of supervisor buy-in. Employees' supervisors don't understand how letting them take off one Friday per month to work in a soup kitchen will help them with their job skills.

Overcome it: It is the employees' job to make the business case for it! They should not leave it up to their supervisors to guess the connection between the volunteer work and their current (or desired future) jobs. The employees must make a succinct and compelling case that describes how the skills gained in the volunteer job will translate to skills they can use in their current or future jobs. Employees might be surprised at how supportive their bosses can be when they see the logic behind it. If not, then they may have to find a way to volunteer during their off-work hours. Finally, a lot of times, we can sell the idea of an experiment more easily than a permanent or long-term commitment, especially because then the results will speak for themselves and fuel future support for our efforts. So employees may need to frame the volunteer-as-development case as an experiment or a contingency agreement and then bring back results that convince the boss to let them continue.

Concern: Role inflation/scope-creep. Volunteers often start with small roles but become enticed to take on more and more responsibilities or to spend more time than they initially agreed to once they're in the roles.

Overcome it: Each of us controls what happens to us. Employee volunteers have to stay focused on their goals and boundaries so as to avoid "scope-creep." It can happen if they let their guard down and if they don't practice mindful prioritization and learn to say no. Volunteers who are overburdened or stretched too thin become burned out, and eventually their performance levels drop. Employees wouldn't want this to happen to them, so they will need to actively protect themselves from it.

Concern: Conflicted developmental goals. If an employees' goal is becoming better at public speaking, volunteering to build a new playground will not help them.

Overcome it: That's true. Employees must identify their development goals and find a volunteer opportunity that will enable them to acquire those specific skills.

Concern: It seems that the employer is making employee volunteering compulsory, either by formal inclusion in personal development plans or through managers asking staff to get involved.

Overcome it: Volunteering is only volunteering if it is voluntary! Corporate volunteering programs must resist the urge to mandate or strongly encourage volunteering and keep it strictly optional. If the organization wants to institute a corporate citizenship strategy that utilizes employees to make investments in the community to create corporate goodwill or for branding or community relations reasons, then the organization must call it that and not paint it as volunteering.

CASE STUDY

Two hundred PricewaterhouseCoopers (PwC) volunteers—partners, staff, and interns from across the United States—traveled to Belize City, Belize, as part of Project Belize, an innovative international experience generated from PwC's broader commitment to youth education and leadership development. The initiative builds on a three-year relationship with schools in Belize City and is primarily focused on financial literacy and environmental sustainability.

The PwC team connected with more than 1,200 students in 10 schools in some of Belize's poorest areas, and focused on four areas of development:

- Hosting a youth financial literacy camp to teach students the basics of banking and budget management.
- Leading a scholar's mentoring program for current and former Belizean students who have received PwC education scholarships.
- Providing financial and technology training to teachers to expand professional capacity.
- Building "Learning Landscape" playgrounds using repurposed materials to reinforce core subjects, social skills, and leadership through games and fun physical activity.

"Project Belize not only makes a lasting intellectual and socioeconomic impact on the children of Belize, but also provides our people an opportunity to demonstrate responsible leadership as they share and develop their skills, mentor children and teachers, and build intercultural competence in a growing global marketplace," says Shannon Schuyler, corporate responsibility leader at PwC. "The program allows us to leverage the firm's intellectual capacity and talent to develop the next generation of leaders—reinforcing our culture of giving back and creating lasting value."

Since 2008, PwC has provided educational support to thousands of students in Belize. In the project's first year, the PwC team refurbished four schools and built a leadership development center that included a library and computer lab. In 2009 and 2010, PwC team members reconnected with hundreds of students in Belize virtually through a letter exchange, a donation drive that resulted in more than five tons of school supplies, and a scholarship program that helped 180 Belizean students pay for their first year of high school. The 2010 program also included a $25,000 donation to the Ministry of Education to fund educational programs.

Project Belize Volunteers' Employee Development Stories
Justin Suissa, Manager in the Security and Privacy Practice

What competencies did you develop? How did you benefit? Team building, flexibility/agility, resilience, creativity and innovation, partnering, problem solving, employee engagement, loyalty to company.

"The experience [building learning landscape playgrounds] was valuable on so many levels. Being in a new culture and working with a team of mixed backgrounds and experience levels allowed me to further develop my team-building skills." Justin was out of his element—construction is not where his expertise lies—and had a tight deadline and clearly defined "deliverables," but many pitfalls and unexpected obstacles to overcome. Having to pull together as a team to build six playgrounds for the children through pouring rain and intense heat and humidity in five days was a challenge that developed his leadership and team-building skills. Justin developed his flexibility and agility competencies to figure out new technical skills in an unpredictable environment—for example, when six of the team's 10 shovels broke in one day, he needed to be flexible and creative to work around these imperfect resources. "While I did not expect it, it was like a learning playground for us, the volunteers. With high stakes and a tough deadline, my teammates and I had to solve problems creatively and let go of preestablished hierarchies in this new environment." It was also a way to network with people across the organization that is otherwise huge and full of silos—"a great opportunity to connect on a new level."

Jack Teuber, Managing Director, Online Marketing

What competencies did you develop? How did you benefit? Stretch—outside comfort zone, leadership, coaching, team building, developing others, agility/flexibility, self-awareness, breaking down positional and geographic silos, leadership bench strength (intern development), employee engagement, loyalty to company.

This experience meant a change in Jack's environment and operational mode—from an unconsciously competent managing director leading a team to a novice middle school teacher in a foreign country, working with children and with a totally new and mixed team of associates and interns. Jack understood that his challenge was "to get out of people's way and encourage them to grow, solve problems, and develop their leadership skills." He developed his ability to collaborate and support others' success through coaching. For example, one of the interns on the team was shy and felt nervous about speaking in public but needed to speak in front of a group of 20 children. Jack was able to develop and coach him rather than removing the responsibility and doing it on his behalf. Jack reflected that he and his teammates all needed to rise to the challenge based on "soft skills" in this new environment—building relationships, establishing empathy, communicating, and partnering. These skills are "extremely important back in the PwC environment because they help us serve our clients better and be better leaders and team players to our colleagues." Finally, the partnering and networking benefits that Jack gained from the Belize experience are tremendous— "the team members still keep in touch after returning home and all of us have developed greater access to and understanding of other areas of the business, which serves to break down barriers, especially the hierarchical ones. Belize affected my self-awareness and has caused me to want to do this for my own team [at home]. It also made me grateful that such an opportunity was available to me."

Mirna Phillips, Executive Assistant

What competencies did you develop? How did you benefit? Cultural awareness, compassion, oral communication, leadership, self-confidence/self-awareness, strong commitment to company/loyalty, stronger community awareness, engagement.

"Poverty in Belize leads to fear in children and mistrust in others; however, after a day and a half of our teaching and working with the children, they opened up their hearts to the PwC staff.

This giving experience in another country has made me more aware that we all experience a need to help each other globally. I also returned eager to volunteer for many more opportunities to help others in my community. I believe that attending and being given the opportunity to participate in Project Belize has opened up an entirely new door of opportunity for me to be more involved in assisting others. I believe I have become more effective in listening and trying to be more interactive in my communication skills with internal and external clients. I have also been more willing to speak up for the executive assistant community and take a more proactive approach to reach out to clients to provide greater value to them and to my manager. I am forever grateful for this valuable development experience."

Key Lessons for Employee Development on a Shoestring

Are you thinking, "This is a costly project. This book is about employee development on a shoestring. Where's the shoestring here?" Yes, this was a big expenditure from a large and generous company, but the same principles can be applied, and the same employee development benefits can be yours for absolutely no money. Volunteering can be done in your local community—no international flights needed. Volunteering can be conducted by individual employees joining other members of the wider community or as a team effort, sending a group of volunteers from the same organization on a volunteer mission. The learning that took place for those Belize Project volunteers could happen in neighborhoods in Los Angeles or Brooklyn. That's what's great about this kind of development method.

RESOURCES

HR.BLR.com. (2005, August 1). *Volunteering Promotes Goodwill, Fosters Employee Development*. Retrieved from http://hr.blr.com/HR-news/ Staffing-Training/Employee-Manager-Training/Volunteering-Promotes-Goodwill-Fosters-Employee-De/

Institute for Volunteering Research. (2004). Community Investment: The Impacts of Employee Volunteering at Barclays Bank. *Research Bulletin*. Retrieved from http://www.ivr.org.uk/Institute+of+Volunteering+Re search%2fMigrated+Resources%2fDocuments%2fB%2fbarclays.pdf

Realized Worth. (2011a). *The Business Case for Employee Volunteering: Case #3. Employee Development*. Retrieved from http://realizedworth .blogspot.com/2011/07/business-case-for-employee-volunteering .html

Realized Worth. (2011b). *Companies Volunteering Globally*. Retrieved from http://realizedworth.blogspot.com/p/global-corporate-volunteering-list-of.html

Wojcik, J. (2008, June 22). Volunteer Work Benefits Employers, Employees as Well as the Community: Companies Supporting Such Programs Viewed Favorably by Job Prospects. *Business Insurance*. Retrieved from http://www.businessinsurance.com/apps/pbcs.dll/article?AID= 9999100025227#

Chapter 4

TAKING TIME OUT: LEARNING ON A SABBATICAL

WHAT IS IT?

A sabbatical is "a planned, strategic job pause during which an employee takes time to travel, do research, volunteer, learn a new skill, or fulfill a lifelong dream before returning to regular work" (your SABBATICAL, 2011). It is not a vacation and can be either paid or unpaid. Sabbaticals typically last from four to 10 weeks, although they can also be up to a year in duration. When we think of sabbaticals, we usually think of them in relation to academicians, because academia was where the concept was institutionalized back in 1880. But that's not the only profession that can and should enjoy this unique type of activity.

The origin of the word *sabbatical* is the Hebrew Sabbath (Shabbat), the day of rest. In Jewish tradition, it is believed that the seventh day should be reserved for rejuvenation, rest, contemplation, and growth so that the person is more refreshed and productive during the other six days of work. The sabbatical (Hebrew: Shabbaton) was introduced as a job break taken every seventh year for the same purpose.

In the context of this book, a sabbatical is a wonderful employee development tool in that it offers employees the opportunity to fully immerse themselves in self-development by stepping out of the daily grind of workday tasks and focusing on their own growth.

I am writing these lines from a sabbatical of sorts in a magnificent historic bed and breakfast nestled in a sleepy village outside Sintra, Portugal. I feel relaxed, creative, and inspired as I feel the breeze from the open window and glance occasionally out to the old castle on a mountaintop on the horizon. My challenge is to develop my writing skills, and I am able to achieve new notches on my writer's belt when I explore a new environment with rich, novel experiences and sensations. I don't produce at the same level, or pace, as I do when I'm seated at my desk, in my office.

Not only is a learning sabbatical intuitively developmental; it can be a powerful qualitative developmental experience as well. Learners can increase their fluency in Chinese, while developing cultural awareness by immersing themselves in Chinese culture, and develop new Chinese contacts to improve their partnering skills. Employees can hone their leadership skills while leading an expedition of volunteers and locals to a remote Peruvian mountaintop village to build a water filtration system. Other learners can improve their oral communication and interpersonal skills by teaching English to would-be entrepreneurs in Nepal. Senior executives can take a month off to sail along the Mediterranean shores and return with a clarified vision and renewed passion for their organizations. Employees who want to develop their entrepreneurial and problem-solving competencies might arrange to shadow six successful people over six weeks and then write a report about their key insights. Other employees may take off for eight months to complete an advanced college degree program. Or they may intern at another company—with a startup, or in another industry, or with one of their clients—to gain new perspectives on old business issues, improve their flexibility, and increase their creativity competencies.

WHO SHOULD TRY IT?

Of course, anyone could try to take a sabbatical, although it's probably most suitable for those who have been on a particular career path for some time—at least a few years. After all, it doesn't make much sense to take a prolonged break when you've only just begun your journey: You are fresh, new, and probably still a novice. You don't need a change of scenery; your work is already new to you.

Additionally, a sabbatical is an investment that makes more sense when the employee is a high-performing contributor whose commitment or competence is not in question. Organizations are not likely to want to invest in people who are troubled in their current roles or seen as slackers.

Is your employee ready for learning on a sabbatical? Invite the employee to complete the self-assessment in Figure 4-1 to find out.

HOW DOES IT BENEFIT THE LEARNER?

Taking a sabbatical can benefit learners in that it allows them to:
- Develop new skills and knowledge.
- Gain a fresh perspective on old problems and issues.
- See the world through a different lens to open new avenues of creative problem solving.
- Gain language skills.
- Increase cultural awareness.
- Increase focus and clarity.
- Solve problems.
- Renew commitment and passion for their organizations and jobs. A recent study found that employees return more committed and more energized from a sabbatical (Journal of Education for Business, 2005).
- Reduce stress and burnout. According to a 2005 survey from the Conference Board, people ages 35–54 work longer hours than their older and younger counterparts, yet only 43 percent are passionate about their jobs; just 33 percent feel energized by their work; and more than 40 percent report feelings of burnout (yourSABBATICAL, 2011).

HOW DOES IT BENEFIT THE ORGANIZATION?

Learners aren't the only ones who benefit from taking a sabbatical. The organization receives:
- Accelerated skill development for key employees.
- Succession planning.

Figure 4-1 ■ Self-Assessment: Sabbatical Readiness

Respond to the statements by placing an X along each spectrum.

1. I am able to create structure and make a plan when there is none.

Not very true of me | Somewhat true of me | Very much true of me

2. I am seen by my supervisor as a solid performer in my current role.

Not very true of me | Somewhat true of me | Very much true of me

3. I don't need other people to show me the way; I can figure it out on my own.

Not very true of me | Somewhat true of me | Very much true of me

4. My colleagues and I have a collaborative team culture.

Not very true of me | Somewhat true of me | Very much true of me

5. [If supervisor/manager] I have the respect and trust of my staff.

Not very true of me | Somewhat true of me | Very much true of me

6. I enjoy venturing to new and unfamiliar places.

Not very true of me | Somewhat true of me | Very much true of me

7. I like being in an unfamiliar setting where I am outside my comfort zone because I always learn something new that way.

Not very true of me | Somewhat true of me | Very much true of me

8. It's important to me to meet my commitments to my organization and customers.

Not very true of me | Somewhat true of me | Very much true of me

9. I like to help develop other people by sharing my expertise with them.

Not very true of me | Somewhat true of me | Very much true of me

10. I have a burning desire to accomplish a goal, but I have not been able to do it because it requires more time and attention than I currently have.

Not very true of me | Somewhat true of me | Very much true of me

11. I like to learn from my experiences.

Not very true of me | Somewhat true of me | Very much true of me

12. If I want to learn something, I figure out how to learn it.

Not very true of me | Somewhat true of me | Very much true of me

- Improved delegation capabilities of leaders.
- Cross-training opportunities for nonsabbatical employees.
- Greater strategic focus for leaders resulting from enhanced delegation abilities.
- Enhanced stretch assignment development opportunities for nonsabbatical staff.
- Enhanced leadership pipeline, building leadership bench strength.
- Greater cultural awareness competencies to improve ability to lead in complex, multicultural, and global business environments. A 2011 study of the global leadership development practices of high-performing companies showed that an increased focus on global and cross-cultural issues was critical to success. It also demonstrated that "cultural components are expected to dominate the new competencies required for global leaders during the next 10 years" (Brotherton, 2011).
- Increased goodwill with employees, clients, and the public.
- Branding as an "employer of choice." The 2011 list of Fortune's "100 Best Companies to Work For" shows 21 companies that offer fully paid sabbaticals, up from 19 in 2010 and 15 in 2009. For example, Microsoft employees are eligible for a paid sabbatical every five years, and all chip-maker Intel full-time employees get a paid eight-week sabbatical every anniversary divisible by seven.
- Improved partnering opportunities within and outside the organization, as well as within and outside the country and current market, creating new strategic network connections.
- Increased employee loyalty.
- Enhanced employee engagement.
- Improved recruiting capabilities. "It's about differentiating yourself," says Rich Floerisch, chief human resource officer at Oak Brook, Illinois–based McDonald's, which offers paid [eight-week] sabbaticals to employees after 10 years of employment. "From what I know, only about five percent or six percent of all companies offer a paid sabbatical. So what

we've done is given our employees—who say they value paid time off more than anything else—a high-value item that differentiates us from competitors" (Silverman, 2006).

- Increased retention of experienced employees.
- Expanded problem-solving resources.
- Ability to leverage existing employees to generate new solutions and ideas outside their immediate job roles.
- New insights into current practices and processes.
- Team and organizational cohesion.
- Increased speed to competence (reduced employee learning curve).
- Culture of collaboration.
- Cost savings from reduced turnover. There is a high cost associated with replacing talent and experience. Sabbaticals can be an effective strategy for keeping people who might otherwise leave the organization due to stress, burnout, or lack of challenging/suitable development opportunities.
- Enhanced ability to innovate.
- A team-based service model.
- Healthy work-life balance.
- Boosted enthusiasm and productivity.
- Improved talent management capacity during a recession.

WHAT COMPETENCIES AND SKILLS CAN IT DEVELOP?

Taking a career break to focus on developing certain skills and knowledge means that the options are almost limitless for the specific competencies employees may decide to work on. Some examples might be:

- Creativity and innovation—employees may choose to work on a special project or creatively solve a business problem during their focused sabbaticals, which would certainly help them develop creativity and innovation skills.
- Cultural awareness—for those who seek to develop better cultural awareness and learn to value cultural diversity and

differences, going into different cultural environments for the period of time away from work is a well-chosen approach.

- Written communication—to develop employees' written communication skills—their ability to express facts and ideas in writing in a clear, convincing, and organized manner—they could choose to take a sabbatical to write an article or a book about a subject of interest.

HOW DOES IT WORK?

How to Prepare

Learners and their supervisors or developers must decide and contract upon the answers to these preparation questions:

- What are the desired outcomes for the sabbatical?
- What measures will be used to assess learners' progress and success?
- How will you get support from leadership for the proposed sabbatical?
- How will learners' work be covered during their absence?
- How will learners' dedicated learning time be protected from abuse or disruptions?
- What supplies are needed? What other resources are required? Who needs to be involved? Whose support is required?
- How will learners record and report an account of their progress and learning as well as their accomplishments?
- How will you celebrate progress and goal achievement?

Ways to Track Progress and Results

Depending on the targeted competencies, employees should use different measures and tracking tools.

- If employees are working on developing cultural awareness, they might find it useful to journal about experiences that raise their awareness of cultural differences, how they deal with those experiences, and what lessons they can draw from the results. The progress they could measure is increasing the number of times they felt competent to deal with the differences effectively or use new cultural awareness to interact more appropriately in different situations.

- If employees are working on enhancing their foreign language skills, you could certainly test those skills using commercially available language tests before and after their sabbaticals to show increased proficiency.

- If, for example, employees are working to develop their writing skills, measuring the clarity or comprehensiveness of their writing products can be a good progress and results tracking method.

- Other ideas:

_____

_____

_____

_____

_____

_____

Implementation Tips

Some important considerations to enhance learners' ability to successfully implement the sabbatical include:

If you need a vacation, take one. Sabbaticals can get a bad reputation when people use the word to describe what is really just a vacation. Sabbaticals as development tools should have a clearly defined strategic purpose. Beware of allowing employees to perpetuate this reputation and misuse the name.

Plan early. Not only will learners need to plan their sabbaticals to fully benefit from them, they must also plan to ensure that their current job responsibilities are smoothly delegated and that those staying behind are able and willing to support their absence. This takes considerable effort and thought and should not be left for the last minute.

Create a business case. Learners need to specifically outline how both they and the organization will benefit from the sabbatical investment, define their sabbatical goals and planned activities to achieve them, and describe in detail how their work will be covered seamlessly by others so that there are no losses to the business during their absence.

Delegate, delegate, delegate. Learners should review all of their current tasks and projects and create a work coverage plan in order to decide how and to whom to delegate their work while they take leave. Especially for those in management roles, a good idea is to begin thinking about ways to delegate some of their work permanently so they can become free to think strategically and spend more time in leadership mode and less time in tactical mode. This action actually benefits the organization by allowing learners to bring higher value to their roles and by stretching and growing the capacity and capabilities of their staff at the same time. This is true succession planning.

Communicate your plan, your goals, and their benefits to others and the organization, early and widely. Learners taking a sabbatical must prepare others as well as build support and encourage champions to prop up their endeavor and sustain its success. They should tell their co-workers, staff, management, clients, and vendors about what they plan to do and how they and the organization will benefit. Ensure that they convey the organization's support of their plan to boost others' acceptance of and support for it. It will build their confidence in the organization to know the organization has confidence in the learner.

Required Resources and Supports
If contact or other information exists about the learner's destination, share it.

Supervisor and peer support—get learners' supervisors on board with the idea of developing skills via a sabbatical. The supervisors will champion the learners' cause and support them with time and other resources. The learners' co-workers and staff must also be encouraged to support them and understand their goals and the plan for a seamless transition of work responsibilities to various colleagues.

Concerns/Downsides

Some of the opponents of this kind of development activity have voiced these concerns:

Concern: Waste and abuse. Learners will not use the time off wisely. They will loaf around and waste it.

Overcome it: First, learners must have a solid plan for how to use the time, even if it includes relaxation and recharging their batteries. Being conscious, deliberate, and mindful in explicitly planning for the sabbatical will help set it up for success. Second, learners must institute strong time management systems to ensure that they stick to the plan and resist detours and derailments. Third, the up-front agreement with the organization for the goals should include some type of deliverable at the end, like a report or a debriefing meeting, to create a little more extrinsic motivation to follow through.

Concern: Senior leadership will not agree to fund it. They will say that "the economy isn't great and we can't afford to pay people for not working. They should just be glad they have a job instead of asking for a paid sabbatical."

Overcome it: For one, it's more expensive to recruit and train new employees. Also, when you look at the big picture, spending one or two months' salary to allow a seasoned employee to take a break and come back re-energized and gratefully loyal is a pretty good investment. Finally, there is always the unpaid sabbatical option that allows organizations to avoid layoffs or cut costs for a short period of time while employees gain valuable development time and achieve their goals.

It's best to approach sabbaticals on a one-by-one basis if they are not already offered at your organization. This allows you to carefully present strong business cases and monitor results and to support the next case with some data. Consider using a pilot—an experiment—to take a slow and smart approach and gather supporting evidence without rocking the boat too much.

Concern: Learners will worry that their departments or teams will function so well in their absence that they will appear unnecessary.

Overcome it: It's not likely to happen, but it's not a good idea for any employee to become indispensable to their organization anyway. Hopefully employees are doing their part to ensure that succession planning and cross-training are taking place anyway, so that they are not indispensable but definitely appreciated and valued.

Concern: Learners' colleagues will be resentful of their sabbatical. They'll believe the learners were just blowing off work during the sabbatical and will resent having had to cover for their duties during that time.

Overcome it: Learners should meet with their colleagues before the sabbatical to ensure that they understand learners' plans and the resulting benefits to the organization and their skills. Then learners should meet with their colleagues (for lunch, for example) as soon as possible upon returning to talk about what they did during the sabbatical, what they learned, and how those development gains will help them contribute better to the team as a result. This important step will help assuage these concerns and reinforce team support and camaraderie.

Concern: My sabbatical will cause a strain on the workloads of my co-workers and staff.

Overcome it: Planning and scheduling, as well as proper cross-training, should eliminate or at least reduce these negative effects. Reframing delegated projects and responsibilities from a developmental lens will help staff see the positive aspects of new assignments. They can even become stretch assignments and be tracked as specific development goals for those employees (for more on stretch assignments, see chapter 6).

Concern: What if learners never return after the sabbatical is over?

Overcome it: Consider setting up the sabbatical agreement with conditions attached. For example, you could have employees agree to reimburse the employer for the full amount of their salary and benefits accrued during the sabbatical period if they leave their job during or immediately after the sabbatical.

You could also institute a sliding scale for what portion of the money must be repaid as time passes (for example, if they leave the organization one year after the sabbatical, they pay 50 percent; two years, 25 percent, and so forth).

Here's something to consider, though: If employees are unhappy, disengaged, burned out, disappointed by being denied a developmental opportunity, or not feeling challenged, they will probably leave anyway. So allowing them to take a sabbatical that will refocus, re-energize, and develop them, as well as create a sense of goodwill and increased loyalty to the organization, might be a good recovery of a potential loss.

CASE STUDY

Cindy Huggett took a one-month sabbatical, and she's glad she did. Cindy is a learning and development consultant, trainer, and author, and she spent her sabbatical completing yoga teacher certification training. As an independent consultant, Cindy spent a long time planning and preparing—in fact, she started six months in advance of her sabbatical to carve out time in her schedule at a point when all client projects were finished or at a point where she could arrange to not work on them for several weeks. She also began letting people know that she would be unavailable during that time. "It was tough to do," says Cindy, "especially turning down some work that would have occurred during that time that I reserved for my sabbatical." There was also the inevitable lingering project that fell past deadline and could have become an obstacle or a distraction from that protected time.

To earn the certification, Cindy had to complete 250 hours of training over a period of four months. She started the online portion before leaving for her sabbatical, which would account for 70 hours out of the total training time. She spent one to two hours each day doing homework during the online portion, working on asynchronous e-learning, and collaborating on a discussion board with others in the program. She completed this portion while still working on client projects. Then came the onsite, hands-on 180 hours of training. She and her cohorts trained in Arizona for 12 hours each day (7 a.m.–7 p.m.) for 15 days. She was in Arizona for two and a half weeks, and also spent one week prior to and after the training workshop decompressing and preparing for the transition to and from the sabbatical.

"It was wonderful!" Cindy says. "I could go on and on about how refreshing and healthy it was for me to do it. Not just because it was an immersion in health, but also to just step away from my work for a while, and to focus on something else. Since returning, I have been more engaged, more productive, recharged, and renewed!"

And, it was "most definitely a learning experience that I can apply to my work. For one thing, being a 'road warrior' in my daily job really takes its toll on my health and body. I have used many of the 'how to stay healthy' lessons I learned during my sabbatical and applied them. As part of the teacher training, we studied healthy lifestyles and nutrition, and I am using them! I've lost 20 pounds of extra weight since beginning the training. I've also used the breathing techniques when under stress, and even talked about them in my class last week (topic was speaking/presentations, and the participants were learning strategies for overcoming nerves)." Time well spent, and development worth gaining!

RESOURCES

Arndt, M. (2006, January 9). Nice Work If You Can Get It: A Handful of Companies Offer Sabbaticals—and Insist That They're Worth the Cost. *Businessweek*. Retrieved from http://www.businessweek.com/magazine/content/06_02/b3966083.htm

Brotherton, P. (2011, August). Top Global Leadership Programs Tied to Business Results. *T+D Magazine*. Retrieved from http://www.astd.org/TD/Archives/2011/Aug/Free/Aug11_Intelligence.htm

Carr, A.E., and T.L.-P. Li-Ping. (2005). Sabbaticals and Employee Motivation: Benefits, Concerns and Implications. *Journal of Education for Business* 80: 160–164.

Cooper, C., A. Weinberg, F. Bond, and V.J. Sutherland. (2010). *Organizational Stress Management: A Strategic Approach*. New York: Palgrave Macmillan.

Gitman, L.J., and C. McDaniel. (2007). *The Future of Business: The Essentials*. Mason, OH: Cengage Learning.

100 Best Companies to Work For. (2011). Retrieved from http://money.cnn.com/magazines/fortune/bestcompanies/2011/full_list/

Silverman, E. (2006, June 2). Taking Leave. *Human Resource Executive Online*. Retrieved from http://www.hreonline.com/HRE/story.jsp?storyId=5495048

yourSABBATICAL. (2011). *Step Out, Step Up*. Retrieved from http://www.yourSabbatical.com

Zimmerman, E. (2008, May 4). The Gainful Way to Use a Sabbatical. *The New York Times*. Retrieved from http://www.nytimes.com/2008/05/04/jobs/04career.html

Chapter 5

TWO CAN DO IT: LEARNING BY MENTORING OR BEING MENTORED

WHAT IS IT?

The word *mentor* originated in Greek mythology. In Homer's *Odyssey*, King Odysseus arranges for his trusted friend and advisor to act as guardian for and to nurture and protect his son, Telemachus, while Odysseus is away to fight the Trojan War. The guardian's name is Mentor. Mentor guides and advises Telemachus on his journey to find out what happened to his father.

Today, we understand the word *mentor* to mean "a trusted counselor or guide" (Merriam-Webster, 2011). There are at least two people in a mentoring relationship, and both can gain valuable new knowledge, insight, and skills as a result of participating in this endeavor.

Mentors are all around you—even some who may not know they are your mentors. To reverse that, you may not be aware of how many people observe and emulate you. Adam Zimet, a business financial manager with the Office of Naval Research who has been in the workplace for a number of years, points out that others observe you and may assume that your behaviors are appropriate for the workplace. "All of us are viewed as mentors by others," he says. "We all need to create our own personal presence; we need to look, talk, think, and act like the leaders we want others to be."

Zimet learned this lesson when he was representing his company at a meeting with senior leaders, most of whom were significantly

Mentors Are All Around Us

I was about six months into my first job out of college, right after the dot-com explosion, and it was hard to find a job. I took a job paying a lot less than what I believed I was worth, and on top of that my boss kept throwing new responsibilities on me with no increase in pay. One day, when I was having dinner with my dad, I started to complain about it, and he told me that in his experience there were two types of employees. The first type would refuse to take on new responsibilities until they were compensated for them. The second type would take on the new responsibilities. He told me that throughout his career he would see both types, but he noticed that the second type was always the group that received promotions when they became available. It is a truism of life that the work comes before the reward—if you wait around and expect to be given the promotion before you get the raise, you will be waiting for a long time. Fathers make good mentors.

Adam Zimet
Business Financial Manager
Office of Naval Research
Naval Air Warfare and Weapons

older than he was. As a nervous habit, he would make wisecracks, albeit polite ones, but wisecracks just the same. After a few of these meetings, his mentor took him aside. She told him that the reason he was representing the company at his tender age was because he had great ideas. However, she went on to say that when he made a joke during a meeting—even if the joke was well received—other people may have perceived him as insincere, a joker, and frivolous. While joking around is good to lighten the atmosphere, there is a time and place for everything. In this case, when Zimet presented an idea, even if it was a good one, the other meeting participants may have been less likely to take it seriously. The company needed him to be respected for his good ideas. "The lesson from this mentor has stayed with me all my life," he reflects. "Mentors can help you see yourself as others see you."

Seventy-one percent of Fortune 500 companies have mentoring programs. A Sun Microsystems study of more than 1,000 employees over five years found that mentors were promoted six times more often than those not in the program; protégés were promoted five times more often than those not in the program; and retention rates were much higher for protégés (72 percent) and mentors (69 percent) than for employees who did not participate in the mentoring program (49 percent; Insala, 2011).

However, mentoring is not limited to those whose employers offer a formal program. In our highly connected world of social networking, new mentoring relationships are emerging as a result of savvy employees (and their employers) making connections and joining groups where they have access to potential mentoring matches. Eager learners and seasoned veterans who are willing to mentor them can easily connect and begin a consensual, mutually beneficial mentoring relationship. Anyone can start a mentoring relationship. And in a global and highly technology-driven world, more and more mentoring is started, and often sustained, virtually.

Mentoring relationships are most frequently conducted on a one-to-one basis. However, mentoring can also take place in groups or one-to-many arrangements. Finally, while most mentoring relationships last for a predetermined period of time (usually nine months to one year), you can also arrange situational mentoring relationships to address a particular learning need or issue.

WHO SHOULD TRY IT?

Below are some of the qualities that are associated with successful mentors and protégés.

Successful mentors:
- are analytical
- are good communicators
- are highly organized
- possess in-depth knowledge of the organization
- have made a strong commitment to training and development
- value action learning
- are committed to being available
- are willing to provide open, honest feedback.

Successful protégés:
- want to acquaint themselves with the company if they are new hires
- seek opportunities for career advancement
- are interested in other areas of the business
- want to expand their leadership abilities
- are successful in previous skill improvement efforts

- are willing to openly share information
- are willing to provide open, honest feedback
- persevere in the face of the ambiguity and awkwardness of learning new skills and making mistakes
- are committed to following through on action items and assignments.

Federal law requires federal agencies to train managers on mentoring employees.

On October 30, 2004, President Bush signed the Federal Workforce Flexibility Act, Public Law 108-411, into law. The act makes several significant changes in the law governing the training and development of federal employees, supervisors, managers, and executives. One major change requires agencies, in consultation with the U.S. Office of Personnel Management (2008), to provide training to managers on mentoring employees.

Ask mentoring candidates to assess their own readiness to perform each mentor behavior in Figure 5-1, see page 75.

Ask protégé candidates to assess their own readiness to perform each protégé behavior in Figure 5-2, see page 76.

HOW DOES IT BENEFIT THE LEARNER?
Benefits to the Mentor

Participating in a mentorship program benefits the mentors themselves because it:

- Renews their enthusiasm for the role of expert.
- Provides a greater understanding of the barriers experienced at lower levels of the organization.
- Enhances their coaching, counseling, listening, feedback, and behavioral modeling skills.
- Increases their generational awareness.
- Provides an opportunity to help someone develop.
- Contributes to the organization's success/future leadership bench strength.
- Allows them to leave a legacy with the organization.
- Increases their support network. (*continued on page 77*)

Figure 5-1 ▪ Self-Assessment: Mentor Readiness

Respond to the statements by placing an X along each spectrum.

1. Help the protégé assess his or her development needs.

| Not ready | Somewhat ready | Definitely ready |

2. Support the protégé in creating a development action plan.

| Not ready | Somewhat ready | Definitely ready |

3. Give the protégé developmental guidance and advice as needed.

| Not ready | Somewhat ready | Definitely ready |

4. Encourage the protégé to stretch beyond her comfort zone with challenging assignments.

| Not ready | Somewhat ready | Definitely ready |

5. Provide both positive and constructive feedback to the protégé in an honest and empathetic way.

| Not ready | Somewhat ready | Definitely ready |

6. Model the way and lead by example.

| Not ready | Somewhat ready | Definitely ready |

7. Share my knowledge of the organization's unwritten rules.

| Not ready | Somewhat ready | Definitely ready |

8. Provide support without removing accountability.

| Not ready | Somewhat ready | Definitely ready |

9. Help the protégé make contacts with senior leaders in the organization.

| Not ready | Somewhat ready | Definitely ready |

10. Introduce the protégé to members of my network outside the organization/department.

| Not ready | Somewhat ready | Definitely ready |

11. Share information about both my success and my failures to help the protégé learn from my experience.

| Not ready | Somewhat ready | Definitely ready |

12. Invest my time and energy in helping the protégé grow.

| Not ready | Somewhat ready | Definitely ready |

13. Help the protégé to learn from her mistakes and challenges.

| Not ready | Somewhat ready | Definitely ready |

Figure 5-2 ■ Self-Assessment: Protégé Readiness

Respond to the statements by placing an X along each spectrum.

1. Assess my own development needs.		
Not ready	Somewhat ready	Definitely ready

2. Create a development action plan.		
Not ready	Somewhat ready	Definitely ready

3. Take the lead on initiating and sustaining the administrative aspects of the mentoring relationship (scheduling, communicating, following up, and so forth).		
Not ready	Somewhat ready	Definitely ready

4. Stretch beyond my comfort zone with challenging assignments.		
Not ready	Somewhat ready	Definitely ready

5. Receive and willingly accept honest feedback (both positive and constructive) from my mentor.		
Not ready	Somewhat ready	Definitely ready

6. Attempt to apply my mentor's advice.		
Not ready	Somewhat ready	Definitely ready

7. Share information about both my successes and my challenges with my mentor.		
Not ready	Somewhat ready	Definitely ready

8. Take responsibility for my own development.		
Not ready	Somewhat ready	Definitely ready

9. Demonstrate accountability for following through on agreements and action items created during mentoring interactions.		
Not ready	Somewhat ready	Definitely ready

10. Honor my mentor's time and energy investment by showing gratitude and goodwill.		
Not ready	Somewhat ready	Definitely ready

11. Approach my mistakes and challenges as opportunities to learn and grow.		
Not ready	Somewhat ready	Definitely ready

- Provides an opportunity to "pay it forward" for mentoring they received in their careers.
- Increases their satisfaction from having an impact on the performance of another.
- Allows for indirect input into decisions or operations of another person/team/department (as result of advice/guidance given to protégé).

Benefits to the Protégé

Participating in a mentor relationship also benefits protégés by providing them with:

- Accelerated learning curve. For example, leaders in a technology firm wanted to accelerate the learning curve for a specific job role. They launched a mentoring program that reinforced classroom training for some individuals and compared them with another group that didn't receive the follow-up mentoring. This study showed that mentoring reduced the learning curve (the number of months it took a new hire to become "fully functional" in the role) by 28 percent, from 18 to 13 months (Insala, 2011).
- A smoother transition into a new role.
- Skill and knowledge enhancement.
- Encouragement to stretch to new goals, overcome challenges, and explore novel career options.
- Career development opportunities.
- New or different perspectives and insights into business issues.
- An opportunity to learn the organization's dos and don'ts and unwritten rules.
- Idea development.
- An opportunity to identify and demonstrate strengths and explore potential.
- An increase in their professional networks.
- Increased professional visibility and organizational exposure (Allen, Finkelstein, and Poteet, 2009; U.S. Office of Personnel Management, 2008).

HOW DOES IT BENEFIT THE ORGANIZATION?

In addition to benefiting the partners in the mentorship, the organization stands to benefit from gaining:

- Accelerated employee learning curves. (See above example.)
- Low-budget employee development. For example, a large automotive manufacturer that was challenged by a growing employee population but flatlined training budgets switched from formal training to mentoring for those professional development activities that could be addressed equally well in this way. This freed up crucial funding that was directed toward other crucial training and development activities, and the organization was able to efficiently use its limited resources, increasing the number of professional development hours it provided to employees without any cost increase (Insala, 2011).
- Increased retention.
- Better employee engagement.
- Cost savings. Reduced turnover and reduced recruiting costs due to lower attrition represent the bulk of the savings.
- Flexible and scalable development tool. Mentoring can be used to meet a wide range of developmental and organizational needs across entire global organizations while still applying a personal context for learning.
- Silo-breaking breadth and depth of employee connections across the organization. Mentoring relationships can and do form across organizational silos to create a broader understanding of the enterprise and its parts.
- Reduced loss of tacit knowledge of seasoned and high-performing employees by encouraging knowledge transfer to up-and-coming protégés.
- Bench strength development. Mentoring develops new leaders and increases the skills and knowledge depth of current leaders. All participants gain a better understanding of the business and increased skills to take the organization to the next level of success.

- Increased diversity and inclusion. Mentoring allows organizations to develop a wide variety of employees and create connections among diverse employees, which increases awareness, understanding, and inclusion of multiple points of view and needs.
- Improved strategic alignment.
- Increased speed to competence (reduced learning curve).

WHAT COMPETENCIES AND SKILLS CAN IT DEVELOP?

Protégés can develop/learn/gain:

- Technical information about the department, organization, or industry.
- Social or informal information about the department, organization, or industry.
- "Lessons learned" from the mentor's experience and history.
- Advice or potential perspectives to consider about a specific challenge.
- Information about career paths and direction.
- Leadership capacity and skills.
- Feedback about their own performance, image, or competence.
- A presence in their professional and social networks, providing access to a wider network of professional colleagues for resources, advice, and support.
- Access to more senior employees and new career opportunities.
- Insight about the organization's unwritten rules or dos and don'ts.

Mentors can develop/learn/gain:

- Leadership capacity and skills.
- Coaching skills.
- Communication skills.
- Knowledge and insights about other employees, teams, departments, and organizations.

- A new perspective on previous or existing practices, problems, or ideas.
- New ideas for performance or process improvement.
- Insights into the perceptions of employees of a different generation or background, or who have different values, styles of working, and professional expertise/experience.
- Access to a wider network of professional colleagues for resources, advice, and support.
- Increased leadership bench strength and boost to succession planning as a result of developing leadership capacity in a protégé.
- Feedback about their own performance, image, or competence.

HOW DOES IT WORK?
How to Prepare
Before you develop a mentoring program or a single mentoring relationship, consider the following questions:

- What are the desired outcomes for this program or relationship?
- How will you measure the program's progress and success?
- What might you or your organization need to do to ensure that this kind of investment of employee time and effort is used prudently?
- How will you or your organization ensure that you communicate the purpose and desired outcomes of this program?
- How will you track and report an account of the mentoring relationship/program's progress and learning as well as its accomplishments?
- How will you celebrate progress and goal achievement?

Mentor Preparation Worksheet

Mentors should prepare for the relationship by considering the following points:

- Name three to five reasons you chose to become a mentor.

  _____

  _____

  _____

  _____

  _____

- Consider motivations that might underlie each reason you have identified. Try to determine your primary motivation for mentoring.

  _____

  _____

  _____

  _____

  _____

- Name one major expectation you have for the mentoring relationship.

  _____

  _____

  _____

  _____

  _____

- Think of a time when you mentored or facilitated another person's learning. What factors positively and negatively affected your efforts?

  _____

  _____

  _____

  _____

  _____

• What are some specific actions that you are able and willing to do to help your protégé?

_____

_____

_____

_____

_____

Protégé Preparation Worksheet

Protégés should prepare for the relationship by considering the following points (adapted from NIH-HHS Mentoring Program, n.d.):

• Name three to five expectations you have for your mentoring relationship.

_____

_____

_____

_____

_____

• Describe why these expectations are important to you.

_____

_____

_____

_____

_____

• Describe your view of an ideal mentoring relationship.

_____

_____

_____

_____

_____

• What is your preferred learning style? (How do you learn best?)

_____

_____

_____

_____

- What are some examples of ways you can gain knowledge from more seasoned or more experienced people?

_____

_____

_____

_____

_____

Ways to Track Progress and Results

The specific goals you set with employees to develop the selected competencies through participating in a mentoring relationship can be tracked in a variety of ways.

- Journaling is one of the best tools for the partners in the mentoring relationship to use to reflect on their progress and insights so they can glean developmental accomplishment.
- Some employees who have pre-mentoring feedback data from a 360-degree assessment or other sources can repeat the data collection at the end of the mentoring relationship to assess how well they progressed in demonstrating their chosen developmental competencies.
- Protégés may choose to measure the number of new contacts they have connected with as a result of the mentoring relationship if they want to work on expanding their networks.
- Other ideas:

_____

_____

_____

_____

_____

_____

Implementation Tips

In a mentoring relationship, the protégé is the driver. Because protégés are the primary beneficiaries of the relationship, the onus is on them to schedule meetings, send agendas, report and follow up on progress and action items, and initiate communication with their mentors.

Preparation optimizes results. Prior to each mentoring session, each protégé should answer these important preparation questions to help focus the session for optimal results (U.S. Department of Health and Human Services, National Institutes of Health, Office of Human Resources, 2011). Employees should forward the responses to their mentors:

- What have I accomplished since our last session? I had # action items.
- What did I not get done, but intended to? What got in the way? What could I have done differently?
- What challenges and problems am I facing now?
- What opportunities are available to me right now?
- What support do I want from my mentor during this meeting?
- By our next session, I commit to do the following actions:

  _____

  _____.

Mentoring should be voluntary, not mandatory. Make every effort to allow the mentor to be selected by the protégé. Both the mentor and the protégé must opt in, mutually commit to the mentoring process, and have a predetermined "divorce plan" should they determine at any point that the relationship is no longer beneficial or effective for any reason. Compelling either party to the relationship can lead to poor adherence, "deadbeat" participation, and ineffective results.

Ensure confidentiality. Mentors and protégés should agree to hold the content of their developmental work together in confidence.

Strong senior leadership support can encourage participation and help reinforce the program's importance. It can help prevent the problems caused by mixed messages that employees receive from unsupportive leadership about where they should put their priorities (usually not on mentoring).

Train both mentors and protégés on how to make the most of the program. Ideally, the training should be segregated—keep mentors and protégés apart so they can feel encouraged and free to ask questions, express concerns, and share ideas with peers.

Required Resources and Supports

Time—mentoring varies in time commitment terms depending on frequency of meetings and the assignments that are agreed to be completed between meetings. If you decide to meet every other week for six months, for one hour each time, you should budget for at least 12–15 hours in those six months just for meetings. However, each party should plan to spend time preparing and following through on action items between meetings, with the heavier preparation workload being carried by the protégé. Plan on approximately two hours of preparation for each hourlong meeting.

Not a lot of money—this development method will cost very little money, if any, except for the cost of the time taken away from other work duties and spent in preparation for meetings, in actual meetings, and on follow-through activities. Occasionally the protégé may be encouraged to purchase books or journals, and sometimes there may be small expenditures for food and beverages if the mentoring meetings occur in a restaurant over coffee or lunch, or while attending professional development events together.

Support tools—consider creating and making available tools that support and enhance the mentoring relationship experience such as goal-setting forms, discussion guides, newsletters, articles, websites, books, and e-learning modules.

Matching tools—some organizations formalize their mentoring programs further by creating (or purchasing and customizing) a matching tool that helps find the perfect pairing for mentors and protégés based on qualities, experiences, interests, and other factors.

Support of peers and leaders—other employees may be called on to support the mentor and protégé by joining in meetings, answering questions, or providing other forms of support. It would be great to gain the support of the direct supervisors of the mentor and the protégé in allowing them to invest their time and energy on the mentorship during work. In addition, consider assigning "mentoring leaders" or "mentoring ambassadors" in each operating division or business unit to provide ongoing program and participant support.

Organizational and infrastructure support—the more robust and structured the organization's support is for mentoring, the more sustainable the mentoring relationship will be. Organizational support can be demonstrated by creating a mentoring program infrastructure that is scalable, strong, and tied to the organization's strategic goals, and that has a demonstrated commitment of and support from senior leadership. Some infrastructure supports include program communication, roll-out support, administration, implementation, tracking technology, connection with organizational objectives, and measurable impact on organizational goals.

Concerns/Downsides

Some of the opponents of this kind of development activity have voiced these concerns:

Concern: Time commitment. Will the mentor have time to meet with the protégé regularly? Some protégés may be concerned that their mentors, especially if they are senior leaders, will be too busy to spend quality time with them. They may be concerned that their mentors will not be able to commit or, worse, will break commitments due to more pressing priorities. They may also be concerned that while meeting with the protégé, the mentor will be interrupted or distracted with other concerns.

Overcome it: This is a potential problem. It can be mitigated by ensuring that mentors consider their readiness to commit in advance of beginning a mentorship. Another way to help avoid this problem is ensuring that mentors and protégés agree and explicitly commit to the frequency and duration of meetings as well as to the ground rules they co-create in the mentoring agreement they both sign at the onset of the mentorship. Finally, if protégés experience a lapse in commitment or follow-through by their mentors, they can bring it up as part of the open and honest feedback and two-way communication that is the cornerstone of the mentoring relationship.

Concern: Perceptions of bias and fairness of mentor. Some might be concerned that mentors will develop a specialized relationship with their protégés that creates an incentive for the mentors to unfairly "stack the cards" in the protégés' favor. It might be perceived by others that mentors give special benefits to their protégés that are not available to other employees, or arrange for unfair opportunities for them.

Overcome it: First, it is important to ensure that there is no truth to these perceptions. Second, sometimes other employees may feel jealous of protégés' access to mentors who might not be accessible to the protégés' peers and other employees on their level. It is indeed a benefit of mentoring—access to, and the opportunity to create a personal relationship and connection with, a person of a more senior level in the organization. However, mentors, protégés, and other leaders (such as the protégé's supervisor) must ensure that they assuage these concerns and clearly communicate what the expectations and practices are in a mentoring arrangement. The more clearly defined the scope is, and the more open and transparent the mentoring partners are about their relationships, the fewer concerns and misconceptions there will be. However, because there is an expectation of confidentiality, mentoring partners must be careful not to disclose any specifics about the content of the mentoring discussions.

Concern: Lack of chemistry between mentor and protégé.

Overcome it: It can happen. To avoid this problem, you can try to create a better match initially by doing a thorough intake to identify strengths, preferences, styles, and experiences had or sought for the two parties involved. If there is a sense that the match is not a good one, encourage the mentor and protégé to give it a try. Sometimes you don't have chemistry at the onset, but you learn to respect, appreciate, and work with another person. This actually encourages growth and development on both ends, which is a positive outcome. Finally, if the mentor and protégé have tried but they're still not feeling a good connection, all mentor partnerships should have an exit strategy or "divorce clause" that they agree to in advance. They are not bound to work together if it's not a good match, and they can agree to separate at any point in the program.

Concern: The mentor doesn't coach and give feedback sufficiently or appropriately.

Overcome it: Mentors should assess their own readiness for providing coaching and feedback prior to engaging in a coaching relationship. But if they just aren't doing this well enough, the organization should help them by providing some performance support such as additional training or other development opportunities so they can bring their skills up to par.

CASE STUDY

Dr. Terri Paluszkiewicz, a physical oceanographer in the Office of Naval Research, is lucky to have had several wonderful mentors who helped her in her career and in her life. She has tried to "pay it forward" by being a mentor, but admits it is harder than it looks. In reflecting on her experiences with her mentors, she thinks the key ingredients are an ability to listen, to reflect back, to convey a path forward with humor, and to convey that sense of care and kindness that lets your mentee know that you are a lifeline. Dr. Paluszkiewicz wishes she had spent the time reflecting before she spent the time mentoring—and maybe she would have been more successful in helping others.

When she looks back, she remembers a lot of small but meaningful moments that helped shape her career. As a woman in the physical sciences, Dr. Paluszkiewicz had mostly only her male counterparts to look toward. As a naïve high school and college student, she thought feminism had opened the doors and she would be received with welcome arms. It took awhile for her eyes to open, and when they did, the mentoring really helped.

In high school, Dr. Paluszkiewicz's physics teacher took great delight in what he saw as an early aptitude for physics and encouraged her forward. He is the only teacher she remembers from all of high school who was encouraging, was supportive, and boosted her motivation. She can't remember his name, but she can remember that he was kind, he had a gentle sense of humor, and the memory comes back as a twinkle in the otherwise dusty, unremarkable haze of high school.

Her advisor in college gave her support throughout and encouraged her to keep true to building her education. Dr. Paluszkiewicz remembers to this day his words of support—after some disappointment or other, he told her, "For some students in high school, everything comes easy, and when they get to college, it's hard. They don't know how to put their back to the wall and fight their way through; they don't know how to learn." His advice to her was not to take discouragement as a measure of ability but to "put my back to the wall and learn and fight my way to success." This advice has helped her through every job she has had and through the long academic road. She tried to pass it to her students, and to her son, but she's not sure she has the timing or delivery right—only time will tell.

Dr. Paluszkiewicz feels as if she wandered through her graduate years like a lost soul until she met one of the most remarkable women in science that she has ever known. This mentor, an émigré from Finland, started well before the easy acceptance of women in their science. She took Dr. Paluszkiewicz under her wing, helped her plan her research, and led gently, but honestly, with determination. While spending time with her, Dr. Paluszkiewicz helped her build her home and saw her travel around the world, writing books about her travels. She showed by example and gentle nudging that you have to ask to receive, and if you ask in just the right way, it will open doors . . . and that is how Dr. Paluszkiewicz met her next mentor.

It may sound odd now, but in her days in graduate school, women were often left out of meetings and parties and introductions, but she learned from her mentors to politely enter and introduce herself, and that led to her first job and dearest mentor: They worked together for years, and he taught her more about work and life. His most memorable advice was: "Let your conscience be your guide" and "When asked, always share." Dr. Paluszkiewicz has used these two guideposts effectively in her life, and if nothing else, they have kept karma balanced.

It's much harder than she thought it would be to mentor; Dr. Paluszkiewicz is not sure she is successful as a mentor. What she remembers about her mentors is kindness, gentleness, and humor. Good advice is valuable, but it is the delivery of that advice that makes it most valuable and the timing of that advice that makes it meaningful.

RESOURCES

Allen, T.D., L.M. Finkelstein, and M.L. Poteet. (2009). *Designing Workplace Mentoring Programs: An Evidence-Based Approach*. Malden, MA: Wiley-Blackwell.

Biech, E., ed. (2008). *ASTD Handbook for Workplace Learning Professionals*. Alexandria, VA: American Society for Training and Development.

Cohen, N.H. (2000). *A Step-by-Step Guide to Starting an Effective Mentoring Program*. Amherst, MA: HRD Press.

Corporate Executive Board. (2004, March). *Mentoring Program Structure and Tools*. Corporate Leadership Council Fact Brief. Arlington, VA.

Drahosz, K.W. (2004). *The Keys to Mentoring Success*. Woodbridge, VA: The Training Connection, Inc.

Emelo, R. (2011, June). Conversations with Mentoring Leaders. *T+D*. Retrieved from http://www.astd.org/TD/Archives/2011/Jun/Free/Jun11_ConversationsWithMentoring.htm

Ensher, E., and S. Murphy. (2005). *Power Mentoring: How Successful Mentors and Protégés Get the Most Out of Their Relationships*. San Francisco: Jossey-Bass.

Insala. (2011). *Mentoring Benefits*. Retrieved from http://www.mentoringtalent.com/mentoring-benefits.asp#tabs

Merriam-Webster. (2011). *Mentor*. Retrieved from http://www.merriam-webster.com/dictionary/mentor

NIH-HHS Mentoring Program. (n.d.). *Preparatory Exercises*. Retrieved from http://trainingcenter.nih.gov/PDF/mentoring/preparatory_exercises.pdf

Phillips-Jones, L. (2003). *The Mentoring Coordinator's Guide*. Grass Valley, CA: CCC/The Mentoring Group.

Schooley, C. (2010, August 6). *Drive Employee Talent Development Through Business Mentoring Programs*. Whitepaper. Cambridge, MA: Forrester Research, Inc.

Stone, F. (2004). *The Mentoring Advantage: Creating the Next Generation of Leaders*. Chicago: Dearborn Trade Publishing.

U.S. Department of Health and Human Services, National Institutes of Health, Office of Human Resources. (2011). *NIH-HHS Mentoring Program*. Retrieved from http://trainingcenter.nih.gov/hhs_mentoring.html

U.S. Office of Personnel Management. (2008, September). *Best Practices: Mentoring*. Retrieved from http://www.opm.gov/hrd/lead/BestPractices-Mentoring.pdf

Zachary, L.J. (2000). *The Mentor's Guide: Facilitating Effective Learning Relationships*. San Francisco: Jossey-Bass.

Zachary, L.J. (2005). *Creating a Mentoring Culture: The Organization's Guide*. San Francisco: Jossey-Bass.

Chapter 6

MOVE AND STRETCH: LEARNING THROUGH ROTATIONAL AND STRETCH ASSIGNMENTS

WHAT IS A ROTATIONAL ASSIGNMENT?

A job rotation assignment is a career development strategy that can be defined as the temporary assignment of an employee to a different job, usually laterally, in another role in the same organization, for an agreed-upon period of time. The rotational job may be in the same team or department, in a new department in the same division or business unit, or in a different business unit or line of service altogether. This temporary new job may allow the employee to use existing skills in a different setting or may require the employee to learn a new set of skills in order to function in the new role. Rotations may commonly be assigned for a "whole job," requiring employees to suspend their current job duties. However, it is also possible to have an employee rotate into a different job for just half-time, for one to four days per week, or for specific periods of the day (such as only afternoons or mornings).

The best way to realize its true potential is to institute a systematic structure and explicitly and consistently articulate the link between the rotational assignment's purpose and organizational strategic goals and business impact. Such a structure supports job rotations that balance the interests of the organization (accounting for employee commitment, attrition rates, and other specific business issues) with employee eligibility and interest (aptitude, competence, and readiness).

WHO SHOULD TRY JOB ROTATION ASSIGNMENTS?

It is possible for almost every role in virtually every organization to be a candidate for job rotation. It is definitely not a development tool that is reserved strictly for leadership development. In fact, it can even be implemented for nonexempt roles such as clerical and administrative support functions. However, job rotation should be implemented in a slightly different way based on the type of role the employee is rotating to and from, as well as the employee's organizational level.

For job rotation of top-level executives, the business problems in various areas must be clearly identified, top management must be involved, and great care must be given to selecting the most suitable people to be shifted from their current jobs to tackle the challenges at hand by considering their individual attributes. Junior- and middle-level executives should select job rotation assignments that pivot around their strengths and attributes and the future roles expected of them. In these cases, the focus must be on exposure in all related areas of their expertise to facilitate their future mobility into higher rungs of management. Finally, for the individual contributor, job rotations may be focused on exposure to multiple aspects related to the work environment or on development of individual competencies or skills.

A study of a 500-employee finance department of one of the world's largest pharmaceutical companies found a strong positive correlation between being in an earlier stage of one's career and the interest and likelihood of participation in job rotation assignments. This study also showed a high correlation between being a high-performing employee and frequency of job rotation assignments.

The study also described job rotation as a way to build one or more of these three types of skills (Cheraskin and Campion, 1990):

1. Business skills (such as organizational awareness, exposure to other areas or aspects of the organization, and understanding how the business operates).

2. Technical skills (such as subject matter expertise of the business unit, for example finance, accounting, and acquisitions).
3. Administrative skills (such as planning, interpersonal relations, leadership, and technology skills).

Self-Assessment: Rotation Readiness

Consider employee and organization readiness for a job rotation by responding to the following assessment.

General Assessment

- The assignment will push the employee just beyond the current comfort zone.
- A plan is in place for meeting the business needs in the employee's current role during the absence.
- The team the employee will join for the rotational role has the capacity to accept and assimilate the employee for the duration of the assignment.
- A plan is in place to ensure a smooth transition from one role to the other.

For Top-Level Executives

- Business problems are clearly identified.
- Top management is involved and supportive.
- This employee is the most suitable person to tackle the specific business challenge (based on the employee's individual attributes).

For Junior- and Middle-Level Executives

- The rotation assignment is well matched to the employee's strengths and attributes and the future roles expected of the employee.
- This assignment provides the employee exposure in an area related to the employee's expertise.
- This assignment facilitates the employee's future mobility into higher rungs of management.

For Individual Contributors

- This rotation exposes the employee to new aspects of the work environment.
- The rotation develops business skills, technical skills, or administrative skills that align with the employee's career development goals.

HOW DOES A ROTATIONAL ASSIGNMENT BENEFIT THE LEARNER?

From job rotation, the learner gains:

- Reduced complacency and boredom of routine.
- Stimulated creativity and new thinking about current role.
- Increased job satisfaction.
- Higher engagement.
- Job enrichment.
- Skill and knowledge development.
- New and increased awareness of personal strengths, competencies, values, management and learning styles, and areas for development.
- Intrinsic motivation to perform caused by newer challenges.
- Career development. An employee who rotates accumulates experience more quickly than an employee who does not rotate.
- A positive attitude toward learning, which leads to learning more efficiently. By having a new position in a challenging rotational assignment, the employee is eager to develop the necessary knowledge and skills to perform in the new position. This motivates the employee to learn during working time as well as during spare time, which leads to greater learning efficiency.
- An increased network of contacts across the organization.
- Increased organizational awareness.
- The ability to introduce creative process improvement ideas resulting from seeing the new job assignment from an unfamiliar perspective as well as seeing the old job with a different lens.

HOW DOES A ROTATIONAL ASSIGNMENT BENEFIT THE ORGANIZATION?

The organization also benefits from job rotation, gaining:

- Employees who bring a new perspective and different way of thinking to their new roles, and then the same benefit to their previous roles, thereby creating opportunities for innovation and problem solving in both areas.
- Lower attrition/increased retention.
- Greater leadership bench strength.
- Alignment of competencies and organizational requirements.
- Rotating employees with a greater positive attitude toward learning and motivation to develop skills, creating more efficient, and therefore lower-cost, learning.
- Employee development that takes place while employees contribute value to the organization as they work productively in their new roles.
- Development of a greater pool of generalists. An employee who rotates accumulates experience in more areas than an employee who does not rotate. So if an employee rotates more frequently, it is easier to train the employee to become a generalist who can add value in a greater number of roles and areas than a specialist. This can greatly enhance the organization's staffing flexibility without needing to add to the head count.
- Greater cross-training.
- Greater knowledge and succession management capabilities.
- Improved cross-organizational awareness and cross-fertilization of ideas and ways of thinking.
- Increased organizational integration and cohesion.

WHAT IS A STRETCH ASSIGNMENT?

A stretch assignment is a task or project that employees perform *usually within their role, but beyond their job description*, that challenges and broadens (stretches) their current skills and capabilities. It forces employees to step beyond their comfort zones and develop new knowledge, skills, and abilities. "Stretch assignments are those that require someone to manage and negotiate change, exert influence over others, and build coalitions. These assignments are highly developmental because they require [employees] to learn new skills in order to be successful in the assignment and they have significant challenges which motivate [employees] to work hard to improve their capabilities," says Professor Paul Tesluk in "Developing Managerial Talent Through Stretch Assignments" (Tesluk and Russell, 2009).

When we align stretch assignments with organizational needs, they can be an extremely effective development tool, especially for those employees who are already highly performing in their current roles. It gives them a challenge without changing jobs, and helps them build new skills in an incremental way and helps to prepare for their next roles or for taking higher levels of responsibility while still in the safety of their familiar roles and environments. Stretching current skills with a safety net can be a great opportunity to grow and learn, especially when the stretch assignment is a time-limited, temporary assignment that lies *just* outside employees' comfort zone and when there are plenty of frequent opportunities to check in with an expert, a coach, or a mentor for feedback and advice.

Below are some examples of stretch assignments:

- Lead or implement a new or important project—a culture change, a new human resource strategy, or a new community project or service closure.
- Organize a conference or lead an important event or meeting.
- Serve on a cross-functional committee within the organization.
- Complete a qualification or significant learning opportunity.
- Work on or manage a cross-cultural team.
- Turn around a failing operation.
- Serve on a task force or special project team that involves an increase in scope (for example, budget, number of staff, or complexity of role).

- Supervise an intern or a volunteer.
- Take an active role in the organization's strategic planning process (Thurman, 2007).

WHO SHOULD TRY STRETCH ASSIGNMENTS?

Every person can benefit from a well-designed, custom-tailored stretch assignment. What's important is that the stretch assignment be targeted to a skill or competency in which employees have reached a level of proficiency in their current roles but are not yet ready to move into the next-level role. The stretch assignment can bridge this gap and prepare employees for the next level of performance or the next rung on their career ladders.

High-performing employees, therefore, are better candidates than struggling employees for stretch assignments. This is a great way to prevent complacency and boredom for those who are already performing well and whose current role may no longer be providing sufficient challenge.

Sometimes a stretch assignment can help address a need for challenge for an employee who is a high-potential candidate for the next role and for whom an appropriate new role is just not yet available within the organization.

Consider your employees' current jobs and ask them to rate their readiness for a stretch assignment using Figure 6-1.

Scoring

If employees' responses tend to be more to the left side of the spectrum (between "Not really" and "Somewhat"), they may be good candidates for a stretch assignment. Their current roles do not present sufficient challenges and opportunities to grow. If employees' responses tend to be more to the right of the spectrum (between "Somewhat" and "Definitely"), they are sufficiently challenged and are probably not ready for a stretch assignment in their current roles (Yost and Plunket, 2009).

Figure 6-1 ▪ Self-Assessment: Stretch Assignment Readiness

Respond to the statements by placing an X along each spectrum.

1. The coming year will bring significant changes.

Not really   Somewhat   Definitely

2. I will be exposed to critical new skills in my current job.

Not really   Somewhat   Definitely

3. My team's and my work will significantly affect the success of the organization.

Not really   Somewhat   Definitely

4. The current job allows me to work closely with senior leaders or the board of directors of the organization.

Not really   Somewhat   Definitely

5. My successes or failures are highly visible in this job assignment.

Not really   Somewhat   Definitely

6. I am held responsible if the team doesn't accomplish its goals.

Not really   Somewhat   Definitely

7. I am pushed to the edge of my comfort zone in the current job.

Not really   Somewhat   Definitely

8. I am faced with significant, never-before-experienced challenges in areas that are important for my development.

Not really   Somewhat   Definitely

9. My current job requires me to significantly expand my leadership capabilities.

Not really   Somewhat   Definitely

10. I have so much work that the only way to get my work done on time is by making tough delegation decisions to get things done through others.

Not really   Somewhat   Definitely

11. I have to influence people and groups over whom I have no direct authority.

Not really   Somewhat   Definitely

12. I have to partner with multiple stakeholders who have different or competing agendas.

Not really   Somewhat   Definitely

13. I have to work with difficult people to get things done.

Not really   Somewhat   Definitely

HOW DO STRETCH ASSIGNMENTS BENEFIT THE LEARNER?

Some examples of how stretch assignments benefit the learner are:

- Increased confidence in abilities and skills.
- Enhanced self-concept as a leader.
- Change in management skills.
- Skills in influencing others.
- Receiving better, more frequent, and more in-depth feedback.
- Leadership development by doing.
- Improved image, visibility, and credibility.
- Development of strategic thinking abilities.
- Enhanced career focus and creation of career development opportunities.
- Expansion of the employee's network, and therefore potential influence, across the organization (if/when assignment offers cross-functional interaction).

HOW DO STRETCH ASSIGNMENTS BENEFIT THE ORGANIZATION?

Organizations benefit from offering stretch assignments in several ways:

- Employee development occurs at a low cost. Employees performing in a stretch assignment are developing and increasing their own potential and output while contributing value to a project or actually filling a head-count position. Studies show that high-performing employees, especially those developing skills for future leadership roles, take stretch assignments seriously and work hard and creatively in their temporary roles.
- There is increased employee retention. Effective stretch assignments can increase the bond between employees and the organization that trusted them with the assignment, and can lead to a higher level of employee commitment as a result.

- Employees bring a new perspective and a different way of thinking to their new roles, and then the same benefit to their previous roles, thereby creating opportunities for innovation and problem solving in both areas.
- Greater leadership bench strength is gained.
- Competencies are aligned with organizational requirements.
- The great positive attitude of stretch assignment employees toward learning and their motivation to develop skills create more efficient and therefore lower-cost learning.
- Employee development takes place while employees contribute value to the organization as they work productively on their stretch assignments.
- Employees gain greater knowledge and succession management capabilities.

WHAT COMPETENCIES AND SKILLS CAN JOB ROTATION AND STRETCH ASSIGNMENTS DEVELOP?

Employees who are placed in developmental stretch and rotational assignments are pushed to step outside their comfort zones and cope with the stress that this kind of uncertainty can produce. However, when the stretch is just outside their comfort zones (not too far) and they have some stress-mitigating supports available to counterbalance the naturally occurring anxiety, they not only gain new skills but also become more adaptive, resourceful, and resilient.

- Cultural awareness/learning to manage diversity—by stretching outside their familiar environs, employees in stretch and rotational assignments are faced with the need to work with people from different cultures (national, gender, racial/ethnic, and organizational, to name a few). They gain important skills in navigating these differences and bridging across cultures. When back at their home organizations or roles, they bring back this widened perspective and are able to strengthen the bridges they began building, as well as create new ones to benefit the organization.

- Flexibility/resilience/composure when faced with difficult situations—to develop this competency, a stretch or rotational assignment that challenges employees to experience a situation that seems chaotic and not within their control might create an opportunity to grow. Employees may be assigned to manage a failing product or project, serve on a task force tackling a controversial organizational issue, or work on the customer hotline.

- Decisiveness—stepping outside their comfort zones on a stretch or rotational assignment will require employees to make decisions, sometimes with limited data or uncertain circumstances. This development method could help an employee to perceive the impact and implications of those decisions and develop good judgment to make sound and well-informed decisions in a proactive way.

HOW DO THEY WORK?

How to Prepare

The level of challenge of the assignment must match the level of readiness of the learner. Prepare for a good stretch assignment by planning a proper match and then following an implementation plan to keep the employee on track. In some cases, it may be necessary to engage a panel of subject matter experts to help employees assess these two factors—especially if they lack the technical expertise in the current role or the stretch assignment's domain area. Here are some questions the employee or this panel of experts should prepare to answer (Macaux, 2009):

- How would this assignment challenge this employee with _____ (insert key outcome competency/skill)?
- What are the specific skills/competencies and the appropriate proficiency levels required to justify assigning this employee to this project?

- How will engaging in this assignment allow this learner to learn and grow?
- Are the necessary organizational conditions present to ensure that this learner has a realistic chance to succeed? Is management prepared to arrange for these favorable conditions?

Other preparation questions include:

- What are the desired outcomes for this stretch assignment?
- What measure(s) will be used to assess the learner's progress and success?
- What might the learner and the organization need to do to ensure that this kind of investment of employee time and effort is protected?
- What, if any, adjustments need to be made to the employee's current role to facilitate the ability to perform in this new role successfully?
- What supplies are needed? What other resources are required?
- What opportunities will we build in for critical reflection and perspective-taking to offset the natural bias for action and results? How will we ensure that there is sufficient time to focus on development and lesson extrapolation?
- How will the employee record and report an account of progress and learning as well as accomplishments?
- How will the employee celebrate progress and goal achievement?

Ways to Track Progress and Results

Consider the key developmental goals and think of measures that would be appropriate for them.

- Employees developing decisiveness should journal about their decision-making process and results. Being able to show increased speed and quality of those decisions will be a great way to show progress and results.
- If employees are taking a stretch assignment to become more flexible in their approach to business practices and problem

solving, they may work on withholding judgment during deliberations and journal their reflections, insights, and results.

- When their development goal is to improve problem-solving skills, employees could track the number of business problems they were instrumental in solving and the cost savings or efficiencies that resulted.

- Other ideas:

_____

_____

_____

_____

_____

_____

Implementation Tips

Avoid implementing job rotation or stretch assignments in a sink-or-swim fashion. In other words, don't just throw learners into the deep end of the proverbial learning pool with no supports and see if they sink or are able to survive. While there is no way to ensure that learners are 100 percent ready for a rotation, there are lots of opportunities to prepare them for success before and during deployment. Sink-or-swim assignments can create too many "false negatives"—the opportunities for failure outweigh the opportunities for success, thereby reflecting in an overly negative way on learners and their capacity or competency. It's not fair and is not a good way to develop people.

Avoid "mother hen" (overprotective) development assignments. The overprotective, doting mother stereotype will not support success in stretch or job rotation assignments. It is too risk-avoidant and can create too many "false positives." These kinds of assignments where nothing could possibly go wrong and nothing is too difficult, or where employees are constantly saved from any challenge or discomfort, don't challenge people sufficiently and are too safe.

The Stretch Zone

Stretch and rotation assignments should push employees to develop just beyond their comfort zone, but no further.

There are three performance zones:

The Comfort Zone—we are fully performing our role. We experience "unconscious competence" and mastery. We are able to perform easily and without exerting great effort. We do not find our work overly challenging anymore. We may be doing just enough to get by if we get too comfortable.

The Learning or Stretch Zone—just outside the comfort zone, this is where we leverage what we know and do well and are able to focus energy on new skills, tasks, or requirements. We are in a state of "conscious competence" where we are building skills but have to be conscious of how we are performing to avoid mistakes and missteps. Our new responsibilities are manageable.

The Panic Zone—if we push employees too far and stretch them beyond their capacity, they may become anxious, confused, and discouraged by so many unknown or unpracticed variables. Here we operate in a state of "conscious incompetence" and even "unconscious incompetence," which feels uncomfortable and which we would like to avoid.

Yes, we could stretch someone too far. And we could stretch someone too little. But the learner has to identify the sweet spot, the Learning Zone, to get it just right.

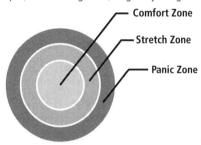

Comfort Zone

Stretch Zone

Panic Zone

Prepare developing learners for participation. This might involve:

- Building self-awareness by assessing strengths, developmental gaps, and developmental requirements or opportunities.
- Developing a specific goal-driven development plan.
- Building in opportunities for critical reflection and perspective-taking to offset the natural bias for action and results with time to focus on development and lesson extrapolation (adapted from Macaux, 2009, 2010).

Required Resources and Supports

Tools of the trade. Ensure that employees have all the tools, supplies, and materials necessary for their rotational or stretch assignments. At minimum, ensure that for a rotation assignment there is desk space where employees can sit during their temporary assignment in the new environment (if it is a desk job, that is).

Create a normative leadership climate that is conducive to development. This might involve:

- Instituting and promoting a generative leadership premise: All leadership stakeholders should see the organization's sustainability, and therefore employee (especially leader) development, as a core governance responsibility.
- Linking development assignments to organizational strategy by defining their specific business impact and strategic significance.
- Ensuring follow-through by creating and adhering to an implementation and oversight structure for all development assignments (adapted from Macaux, 2009, 2010).

Build a community of practice of stretch and rotational assignment alumni. This community can be hosted online, with opportunities for group interaction and support.

Concerns/Downsides

Some of the opponents of this kind of development activity have voiced these concerns:

Concern: Job rotation is viewed by some as just another job transfer. Even worse, it is sometimes applied as a means of punishing poor performers, "playing politics," or going through the motions without regard to business impact.

Overcome it: Job rotation can definitely lose its potency as a viable and desirable development tool when it is applied as a rote action detached from its link to organizational strategy or business impact. The only way that job rotation can be seen as a truly strategically significant organizational tool is when it is implemented with a mindful focus on its connection to positive outcomes that benefit the organization as well as the individual or department.

Concern: Putting an inexperienced employee in a key role puts the business operation at risk. People who are rotated into a role or given a task that is a stretch for their current skill set are not going to perform as proficiently as those who have already mastered that role. Therefore, the work may not be completed in an error-free, top-quality, maximum-efficiency way.

Overcome it: Yes, there is some risk associated with putting work in the hands of less-than-proficient workers, but management can mitigate this risk by introducing what researchers call moderating variables (Figure 6-2, on page 111). Moderating variables can help reduce the steepness of a learner's learning curve. They include the availability of feedback, coaching, and other structured development support programs (see sidebar, on page 111).

Concern: Putting an inexperienced employee in a key role creates a lot of stress for the learner and brings about a sense of being overwhelmed. This feeling can overload the learner's ability to be resilient and cope with the new role, thus risking a fear of performance, and potentially lead to failure. The challenge may be so steep that instead of the initial motivation it sparks, it can lead to desperation and defeat.

Overcome it: To mitigate this risk of overload and being overwhelmed, the moderating variables mentioned above must be introduced. With the right supports, research shows that the steep learning curve that leads to diminishing returns in skill development is reduced so that the learner remains in the "challenging yet doable" range (see Figure 6-2, on page 111).

Concern: Stretch assignments are not scalable. If the organization wants to develop the leadership skills of 15 high-potential employees, it may seem easier to register them all for one leadership development workshop than to create 15 stretch assignments or find them 15 job rotation roles.

Overcome it: Seminars and workshops are indeed more scalable development tools that have their proper place in any employee development strategy. Rotational and stretch assignments should complement, not replace, these classroom-based (or online) training events. There are many benefits to on-the-job learning that cannot be realized in a learning event like a seminar or workshop. Organizations that seek to maximize employee potential and leverage development opportunities presented in the daily work environment must look beyond these seemingly simple and insufficient solutions to present a more robust learning and development range of offerings. In addition, by creating a solid, structured, repeatable program template, organizations can, in fact, create a relatively scalable development program for these kinds of assignments. Many of the structures, processes, and even projects themselves do lend themselves to repetition with new learning candidates.

Concern: Lack of leadership support for the program.

Overcome it: Even though a lack of leadership support makes it much more difficult to implement any program, there is always the power of operating locally and creating a track record of positive results that will build support in the future. One suggestion is to work on identifying and cultivating "Advocates" and "Champions," one at a time. Eventually, they will build a grassroots support network that will engender wider-ranging, deeper, and stronger leadership support.

Concern: Job rotations spin quickly out of control—it becomes hard for the organization to keep up with the constant need to fill jobs that become open as a result of successive rotations. This high rate of rotation creates a ripple effect that is disruptive to continual operations.

Overcome it: Organizations must guard against this situation by building strong succession management practices. In fact, rotation may allow organizations to run lean on staff while developing employee skills at the same time by prudently and strategically using job rotation (and stretch assignments) to address talent needs nimbly throughout the organization.

Concern: Won't temporary, short-term job rotation and stretch assignments cause the workforce to become "jacks of all trades, masters of none"?

Overcome it: It is true that job rotation and stretch assignments can build more generalists. However, organizations can limit any liability this can create by modulating the duration of the assignments and rate of rotation to ensure that sufficient depth is achieved in addition to the breadth that can naturally result. Another possible focus can be to ensure that the organization also creates assignments that generate greater depth and skill or knowledge specialization by building specialization tracks in which employees rotate into roles that are related to each other and drill down into the same skill set, rounding out these skills and creating fuller mastery of them.

According to William Macaux (2010), "The relationship between the level of challenge of a stretch assignment and the gains in leadership skills obtained from the assignment is curvilinear." The more challenging the development assignment is, the greater the skill gain is—but only up to a point. Once employees go past a certain level of challenge, the curve turns, and getting more challenges from that point on brings on diminishing returns in skill development (curve B–C in Figure 6-2). We are motivated to grow and learn as long as the challenge is manageable. Otherwise, we start to feel overwhelmed and stressed.

However, there is a way to prevent the steep drop in the curve by introducing what Macaux (2010) calls *moderating variables* (curve B–D in Figure 6-2), which include the "availability of feedback, developmental coaching, and a structured program to support development" (such as action learning).

Figure 6-2 ▪ Moderating the Effect of Developmental Challenge

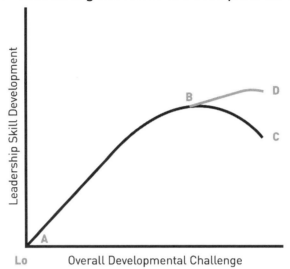

Source: Macaux (2010).

CASE STUDIES

One particular story of an employee of a large technology corporation told her story of how appreciative she was that her employer was so accommodating of its employees' development needs. She described how she wanted to move from her current 24-hour-per-week job-sharing staffing consultant role to a full-time arrangement. She had expressed an interest in exploring program management responsibilities with the company's staffing systems. It just so happened that the team needed some extra help. It was the impetus for a win-win solution: She was offered a stretch assignment to help with staffing systems for eight months. The staffing team members get to have an employee helping them out who is already familiar

Moderating Variables— Support Programs

Macaux (2010) identifies these moderating variables:

- availability of feedback
- self-awareness support tools
- coaching
- mentoring
- peer support group
- reading materials
- online learning modules
- action learning group.

with the organization and the systems, and this employee is able to experience the role and gain new skills without fully committing to a career change.

At the end of the temporary assignment, she will return to her previous role, unless she decides to explore similar opportunities in a permanent arrangement elsewhere in the organization or, of course, shift to a permanent position in the team she helped if such an opening is available at that time. This employee expressed that she felt fortunate to enhance her skills, network within the organization, see other team dynamics, understand different roles, and take on new challenges.

An employee of another well-known Fortune 100 company told her story of volunteering for a stretch assignment role in one of the company's large Europe-based IT programs to learn more about the system and then be able to support its implementation in another location later. This particular assignment allowed this employee to stretch her leadership and language skills as she did not speak the local language very well when she was transferred to this location. She needed to stretch quickly and develop skills to give a presentation in the local language within six weeks of arrival. She also learned conflict management and interpersonal influence skills by having to navigate the political minefield of being seen as an outsider and working on a multiparty project with a competitive, noncollaborative culture. Finally, she gained crucial leadership skills when she sought a team leadership role where all team members were locals, varying greatly in age, and hailed from different organizations with different expectations and priorities but with a stake in the program. This employee admits that this assignment was quite stressful but rewarding because she learned fast and developed in multiple crucial leadership and language competencies that bolstered her subsequently successful career with the company.

RESOURCES

Center for Creative Leadership. (2010). *Development Planning Guide: Benchmarks*. Retrieved from http://www.ccl.org/leadership/pdf/assessments/BenchmarksDevelopmentGuide.pdf

Cheraskin, L., and M.A. Campion. (1990). Study Clarifies Job-Rotation Benefits. *Personnel Journal*, *75*(11), 31–38. Retrieved June 25, 2011, from www.peoplehrforum.com

Colvin, G. (2008). *Talent Is Overrated: What Really Separated World-Class Performers From Everybody Else*. New York, New York: Penguin.

Macaux, W. (2009, October 6). *Making the Most of Stretch Assignments*. Generativity LLC White Paper. Retrieved from http://www.generativityllc.com/Whitepaper-Making-the-Most-of-Stretch-Assignments.pdf

Macaux, W.P. (2010, June). Making the Most of Stretch Assignments. *T+D*. Available from http://store.astd.org/Default.aspx?tabid=167&ProductId=21240

Tesluk, P., and J.E.A. Russell. (2009). Developing Managerial Talent Through Stretch Assignments. *Academy of Management Journal*, *10*(2). Retrieved from http://www.rhsmith.umd.edu/research/ras/Oct2009/ManagerialDevelopment.html

Thurman, R. (2007, October 3). *The "Stretch Assignment."* Retrieved from http://www.rosettathurman.com/2007/10/the-stretch-assignment/

Yost, P.R., and M.M. Plunket. (2009). *Real Time Leadership Development*. Malden, MA: Wiley-Blackwell.

Chapter 7

TEAM EFFORT: LEARNING IN SPECIAL TEAMS

WHAT IS IT?

A special team is typically a cross-functional group of people with varied levels of skills and experience, often from different organizational units, brought together to accomplish a task. Special teams are usually temporary, ad hoc teams that dissolve once their specific goal is accomplished, as opposed to permanent work teams that perform set recurring functions in an ongoing fashion within an organization.

Several names exist for special teams, some of which are quite similar in function. We can trace the origins of the different names and the distinctions that may have existed in the past, but the reality is that names are often used interchangeably, depending on the organizational custom. For the purpose of this book, they will be lumped together as a single development method. Examples of special team types include task forces, working groups, project teams, ad hoc committees, tiger teams, problem-solving teams, workouts, and strategic focus teams.

These special teams are created to solve an organizational problem, to improve a process, or to accomplish a task that requires breadth and depth of knowledge, skills, and experience. These teams may use action learning as a process to solve problems.

A similar type of team with a different purpose is a learning team, also an ad hoc team whose members focus on a common learning goal instead of a business issue or problem resolution as their goal.

By participating in the team's problem-solving or learning process, employees are stretched to think creatively about problems and work collaboratively across boundaries to reach decisions that improve the organization in some way. In that way, the experience is developmental for participants.

Action Learning

Action learning is a method for solving complex problems that often appear unsolvable. In addition to solving problems, action learning helps develop its participants "because its simple rules force participants to think critically and work collaboratively, and because the group's coach, the action learning coach, assists group members to reflect, not on their problem solving, but on the elevation of their group functioning and on examples of their leadership skills" (World Institute for Action Learning, 2011). Sometimes a series of one-time action learning meetings are called workouts.

Washington, D.C.–based law firm Howrey uses action learning teams as part of its employee development strategy. Several teams, each made up of five to seven first-year associates along with a sponsoring partner and an advisory senior associate, are assigned a project related to an important firmwide issue. Associates then are encouraged to contribute in areas to which they typically would not be exposed. For example, because most of Howrey's clients are multinational firms, a recent team assignment revolved around the Foreign Corrupt Practices Act. The team had to come up with a way to share guidelines and best practices with Howrey attorneys and clients in other countries in order to ensure that clients comply with the act.

Each team has 90 days to understand the needs identified by its sponsoring partner, conduct research, and create an appropriate solution. Throughout, team members receive feedback on their interpersonal, communication, organization, meeting management, leadership, and client relationship skills from their peers.

Peer learning allows participants to receive a greater amount and less intimidating form of feedback compared to what they receive from partners in the course of daily work. Additionally, by having to provide feedback to their teammates regularly, associates develop skills in both giving and receiving feedback (Bock and Berman, 2011).

You can also build the special team and action learning approach into executive development programs. It infuses participants with context and relevance through its "high-stakes, high-reward strategy" (Blanchard and Witt, 2010). It allows them to experience a model for improving organizational effectiveness while enhancing their individual leadership skills. Participants in a FDIC-based executive cohort action learning team reported that having the opportunity to try out the method on a real and significant organizational issue built their understanding of the process and convinced them that this tool can serve them well in resolving their own issues later (Lanahan and Maldonado, 1998).

At Skanska, a construction and project development company, participants in an executive development cohort program are split into five teams of seven and given a large action learning project. Each group has two months to work on a different business issue identified by the company's senior leadership. The teams have a C-level team sponsor and are asked to present their final recommendations to the top 24 members of U.S. senior management. The senior leaders then decide which projects to implement, in full or in part. Of executive respondents to a 2008 study, 83 percent said they learned new skills that both were relevant to their work and produced results (Blanchard and Witt, 2010).

WHO SHOULD TRY IT?

Special teams are usually composed of diversified representatives from certain business units or functions, for example, and ensure a complementary mix of skills and knowledge of team members. Therefore, employees are selected for membership in special teams based on their specific set of skills, knowledge, or experience vis-à-vis the team's needs.

This kind of learning opportunity is well suited for solid performers and self-motivated employees who are ready to stretch beyond their current skill levels and outside their comfort zones. This kind of development is one example of a stretch assignment (see chapter 6 for more on stretch assignments).

You should ensure that employees who are interested in joining a team, or who are invited to join one, have the capacity to perform this additional role successfully along with their existing role. If employees already have an overload of work, either some of their work should be reassigned or they should consider waiting before joining a special team.

Self-Assessment

Consider the employee's and the organization's readiness for special teams by responding to the following assessment.

General Assessment

- Serving on this kind of team will push the employee just beyond the employee's current comfort zone.
- A plan is in place for prioritizing and balancing the employee's current workload to allow the employee to successfully serve on the team.
- The team the employee will join has the capacity to accept and assimilate the employee.

For Top-Level Executives

- Business problems are clearly identified.
- Top management is involved and supportive.
- This employee is the most suitable person to tackle the specific business challenge (based on the employee's individual attributes).

For Junior- and Middle-Level Executives

- The team assignment is well matched to the employee's strengths and attributes and the future roles expected of the employee.

- This team assignment provides the employee exposure in an area related to the employee's expertise.
- This team assignment facilitates the employee's future mobility into higher rungs of management.

For Individual Contributors

- This team assignment exposes the employee to new aspects of the work environment.
- The team participation develops skills that align with the employee's career development goals.

HOW DOES IT BENEFIT THE LEARNER?

Participation in special teams provides learners with:

- Improved problem-solving and decision-making skills.
- Increased creativity and innovation in approaching problems.
- Improved team-building and partnering skills.
- Ability to apply a problem-solving model.
- Facility with use of the action learning model that they can apply to their own issues.
- Increased ability to positively affect the organization.
- A broadened network of cross-functional contacts.
- Greater visibility with senior leadership.
- Opportunities to gain and demonstrate leadership skills.
- Enhanced strategic thinking and greater organizational perspective.
- Better solutions to issues they've tried unsuccessfully to resolve in the past.
- Greater loyalty and commitment to the organization.

HOW DOES IT BENEFIT THE ORGANIZATION?

The organization gains:

- Solutions to real, complex, and vexing business issues.
- Opportunity for development for high performers.

- More skilled employees.
- Increased engagement and retention of high-performing employees.
- Better partnering between different organizational functional areas.
- Replicable tool for fast and effective decision making.
- Improved business processes—streamlined or cost-reduced.
- A low- or no-cost employee development opportunity.
- Better, quicker decision-making capabilities of senior leaders by presenting them with comprehensive, reliable analysis and strong recommendations.

WHAT COMPETENCIES AND SKILLS CAN IT DEVELOP?

Just as there are many different types of special teams an employee could join and many topics or problems these teams focus on, so are there many options for the competencies that could be developed as a result of serving on such a team. Here are just a few examples to get the ideas flowing:

- Strategic thinking—this competency allows an employee to determine objectives, set priorities, and anticipate potential threats or opportunities. Serving on a special team can be a practical way to develop it.
- Partnering—by serving on a special team, employees can develop networks and build alliances, as well as engage in cross-functional activities and collaborate across boundaries.
- Team building—clearly, by being part of a team that has a specific purpose and is expected to work cooperatively to deliver on its goals, employees could improve their team-building abilities.
- Problem solving—developing this competency allows employees to identify, analyze, and provide solutions to individual and organizational problems. Serving on a special team facilitates this kind of development.

HOW DOES IT WORK?

How to Prepare

For general special team preparation, supervisors should:

- Choose team members who have the right mix of complementary skills and expertise.
- Clarify goals and desired outcomes.
- Define timelines and actions to accomplish the goals.
- Identify the roles and responsibilities of team members. Is there a designated team leader, or will the team be self-directed? Assign a recorder, facilitator, and timekeeper, at minimum.
- Identify and obtain the necessary resources.
- Periodically evaluate the functioning of the team and make course corrections if the team is not on track to meeting its goals by the assigned deadline.

To prepare for action learning, supervisors should:

- Clarify the objective of the action learning group.
- Convene a cross-section of people with a complementary mix of skills and expertise to participate in the action learning group.
- Identify an appropriate champion and sponsor for the team. This can be a role for a stakeholder who needs to be involved but doesn't have the prerequisite expertise to merit a role as a team member.
- Ensure that relevant and useful data are available for the team members before they meet (they may be the ones gathering it as prework).
- Arrange for the facilities, equipment, and materials/resources necessary for the team meeting.

Supervisors may also ask these preparation questions:

- What are the desired outcomes for the learner as a team member? For the team?
- What measures will be used to assess the learner's and team's progress and success?

- What might you, the learner, or management need to do to ensure that the investment of employee time and effort is well spent?
- How will you communicate the purpose and desired outcomes of this team?
- What will you or your organization do to protect the team's ability to meet and perform its work without disruption?
- What supplies are needed? What other resources are required?
- How will the learner and other team members support ongoing customer service coverage and maintain ongoing business processes and operations during this dedicated learning time?
- How will the learner and the team record and report an account of their progress and learning as well as accomplishments?
- How will the learner and the team celebrate progress and goal achievement?

Ways to Track Progress and Results

Measures will depend on the competencies and goals set for employees.

- If employees want to develop their partnering skills by serving on a cross-functional team, they could show the successful completion of the team's goals as evidence of working effectively across boundaries. It would also be possible to survey the other team members about their satisfaction with their interactions with action learning employees to gauge their partnering effectiveness.
- If improving problem-solving abilities is the employees' goal, they could journal about the various experiences and insights they have during the team's problem-solving process and draw lessons learned. They could measure increased ease with developing solutions by quantifying those journal insights. The quality of the team's final report, recommendation, or

solution can also be used as a measure of employees' problem-solving improvement as one of the contributors.

- Other ideas:

_____

_____

_____

_____

_____

_____

Implementation Tips

Follow a sequence of steps to ensure action learning success. Ready to try action learning? Here are the basic steps to follow:

- Hold initial meetings to analyze the issues and identify actions for resolving them.
- Return the group to the workplace to take action.
- Use subgroups to work on specific aspects of the problem if necessary.
- After a period of time, reconvene the group to discuss progress, lessons learned, and next steps.
- Repeat the cycle of action and learning until the problem is resolved or new directions are determined.
- Document the learning process for future reference. Record lessons learned after each phase of learning.
  Note: In some cases, the team presents its recommendations to senior leaders who decide which recommendations to implement and then prepare to get implementation started right away. In other cases, the team itself has the sufficient authority to decide and act.

Action learning can fail if participants perceive that it is only a training gimmick. The key to the success of implementing an action learning team is to tie the work the team does to the current or future business strategy and objectives. It must also be focused on teaching skills that participants are able to immediately apply; they need to

123

see how what they practiced during the action learning forms tangible, business-relevant experience (Blanchard and Witt, 2010).

Executive support is crucial for success. When the sponsor demonstrates that the issue is important, the team is more likely to work harder and produce high quality results. If the sponsor or top leadership does not lend credence to the work of the team, the team will become unmotivated to put real effort into it, feeling like it's a futile exercise or not worthwhile. This is especially true when the team's recommendations aren't taken seriously or implemented. Implementation is the most important part of this process.

Required Resources and Supports

Technology—meetings usually require a laptop computer and an LCD projector. Having access to a printer is a big boost to productivity and efficiency.

Supplies—similar to supplies used by a typical training session, special team supplies include flipchart pads and easels, markers, tape, pens, and so on.

Logistics—facilities, refreshments if appropriate, and scheduling supports are typical logistics.

Human resources—sometimes during the working session the team needs additional information, so identify people who can serve as expert consultants to the team on an on-call basis for certain topics.

Strong facilitator—consider having a professional facilitator help the group stay on task, pull out learning points, make collaborative and inclusive deliberations and decisions, and work through conflicts productively.

Concerns/Downsides

Some of the opponents of this kind of development activity have voiced these concerns:

Concern: It's too much work to both serve on this team and continue my daily duties.

Overcome it: Sometimes that is true. It will be important to help the employee assess whether there are tasks and projects that can be delegated to others, postponed, or renegotiated. The employee's supervisor should show support by removing obstacles and helping the employee prioritize and balance the workload.

Concern: We did all this work on our team, and nothing was ever done with our recommendation.

Overcome it: Implementation is the golden key to the future success of this or any other team. When the team's work is not applied to real business issues, the team's work is cast into question, and the team members are likely to become deflated or demoralized and disinterested in continuing their work. Others in the organization hear this and are deterred from participating in similar teams in the future. Senior leadership must support the initiative visibly and consistently up to and including implementation, removing obstacles, and championing the cause along the way.

Concern: The team was assigned a problem that is too big— beyond its ability to affect or influence.

Overcome it: It's important to assign a topic that is workable— aggressively challenging yet attainable. The sponsor and decision makers must have sufficient authority to make decisions about the topic.

CASE STUDY

Manuel Figallo works for a small consulting firm as a data architect and manager. He recognized that he needed to develop his technical skills with SAS, a software program that is key to moving into a new level of proficiency at work. When he researched the options, he realized that most training for SAS certification involved attending an off-site SAS training at a SAS Training Center. He looked into it and found that those programs took a cookie-cutter approach, were not necessarily of high quality, and would not be targeted to his level but rather would be provided at the lowest common denominator level, which would not satisfy his learning goals.

125

Manuel decided to take a different certification route: He decided that he would form an independent learning cohort that would work together to prepare for the certification exam. "It was a bit against the grain to approach things in this way," admits Manuel, but with a grassroots group, he recognized that he would be able to totally customize the study approach to make it "really relevant for us." So he formed the SUG (SAS Users Group) Certification Review and recruited five other members to join him. The group met weekly, and during each meeting, a different member took the lead on guiding the group in study of one of 21 chapters in the study guide. They had a specific mission and goal: to prepare for, and pass, the SAS Certified Base Programmer exam. The group members had to meet during lunchtime because they were not allowed to use their billable time to study. However, their employer supported them by supplying them with the study materials, paying for the exam, and encouraging their efforts.

The group's working approach of sharing the leadership and responsibility for preparing a lesson plan worked great. Each member was able to develop by leading some of the sessions. Members were able to take what would otherwise be very dry content and make it easier to learn in a supportive community of peers. They used their own data to customize their application of the material and make it more meaningful and relevant. And the tacit accountability ensured that the leader prepared an outline for the chapter to help review it and lead the session.

Finally, Manuel took the initiative to evaluate and measure progress to ensure the group's effectiveness. He asked the group members to complete a short satisfaction survey at the midpoint and again at the end of the group's process. He used this survey to produce a status report for his employer, who at first was somewhat resistant to the idea, with an assurance that the group was successful and on track, reinforcing the employer's decision to support the group (see Figure 7-1).

Not only did the members of this self-directed, grassroots study group pass the SAS certification, but they also won a recognition award from their employer for creating and running the successful and innovative group.

Figure 7-1 ▪ Manuel's SUG Assessment Survey

Please rate the study group using the following options:

| 5: Strongly Agree | 4: Agree | 3: Neutral | 2: Disagree | 1: Strongly Disagree |

1. So far, I am satisfied with the study group.

2. So far, the learning event has met its stated objectives to share knowledge effectively and to help me do my job better.

3. So far, the amount of content covered is appropriate for the learning event.

4. So far, I have a better understanding of SAS.

5. I would like to see more of these activities in the future (for example, for EBI).

6. Regarding the study group, I would like to say . . . (suggestions on improving it are welcome).

RESOURCES

Blanchard, S., and D. Witt. (2010, April). *Action-Packed Learning. Talent Management.* Retrieved from http://talentmgt.com/articles/view/actionpacked_learning

Bock, H., and L. Berman. (2011, February). Learning and Billable Hours—Can They Get Along? *T+D.* Retrieved from http://www.astd.org/TD/Archives/2011/TOC/1102FebTOC.htm

Lanahan, E.D., and L. Maldonado. (1998). Accelerated Decision Making via Action Learning at the Federal Deposit Insurance Corporation (FDIC). *Performance Improvement Quarterly* 11: 74–85.

Organizational Learning Strategies. (n.d.). *Action Learning.* Retrieved from http://www.humtech.com/opm/grtl/OLS/ols2.cfm

World Institute for Action Learning. (2011). *The Certification Organization for Action Learning.* Retrieved from http://wial.org

Chapter 8

TEACHING TO LEARN: LEARNING BY TEACHING OTHERS

WHAT IS IT?

"To teach is to learn," or so goes the old Japanese proverb. And if you want to help your employees develop quickly, give them an opportunity to teach others. It could involve taking a role of co-presenter or co-trainer at one of your onsite training programs, or it could be helping employees find an opportunity to design, develop, and present a short workshop to their colleagues. One of the best ways to leverage this idea is by structuring a brown-bag or lunchtime training series run for and by employees.

Many office workers are familiar with the term *brown-bag training*. The idea behind the traditional brown-bag session is that a training presentation or event occurs during the traditional lunch hour in the workplace. Employees are invited to attend for free, bring along their lunch (in a brown bag or any other container, hence the name), and learn during their lunch break. The presentation may be conducted by a fellow employee, an organizational leader, a vendor, or an external consultant or trainer brought in for particular topical expertise.

This method is different from traditional training in that it is short in duration (usually 45–90 minutes) while usual training courses last between a half-day and a full week on average. Also, brown-bag sessions don't usually require a lot of administration or tracking as do formal training classes. It is a good way to use a short timeframe to learn about a topic in a relaxed atmosphere with little to no performance anxiety because the learning is usually not measured or tracked.

And while employee development occurs by attending a brown-bag session presented by any of the types of presenters previously listed, double employee development can occur when the presenter is also an employee or a leader in the organization because the process of designing, developing, and delivering the session is inherently developmental. Therefore, since participation in a brown-bag session is not really an outside-the-classroom development method, this chapter will focus on the latter form of brown-bag learning: lunchtime presentations designed, developed, and delivered by employees or leaders to their co-workers.

Topics for brown-bag sessions can span a wide range of subjects. Here are a few examples of what brown-bag learning sessions can be about:

- Products or services.
- Business processes.
- Business problems.
- Vendors or competitors.
- New ideas or innovative solutions.
- Success stories.
- Mistakes made and lessons learned.
- Unrelated experiences that have learning points that can be applied in the workplace.

WHO SHOULD TRY IT?

Any employee, at any level, from any department, can initiate, design, develop, or present a workshop or a brown-bag session. Employees may be experts on a topic and want to share their expertise with colleagues, or may have a story of a challenge they faced and overcame so others can also benefit from the lessons they learned. Or, employees may be interested in learning more about a topic, an issue, a product, a process, or anything else that may also be of interest to others in the organization, and might use the brown-bag session as a catalyst for learning as they prepare to teach about it. Finally, this is a great developmental opportunity for employees whose development goal is to become better presenters or trainers, in which case the subject doesn't even matter, because the benefit to the presenter is in the preparation for and delivery of the presentation itself.

Is your employee ready to take up teaching as a development method? Let your employee complete the self-assessment in Figure 8-1 to find out.

Figure 8-1 ▪ Self-Assessment: Presenter Readiness

Respond to the statements by placing an X along each spectrum.

1. I like to help develop other people by sharing my expertise with them.		
Not very true of me	Somewhat true of me	Very much true of me

2. I have ideas, examples, or stories that other employees would find useful and interesting.		
Not very true of me	Somewhat true of me	Very much true of me

3. I want to develop my public speaking skills.		
Not very true of me	Somewhat true of me	Very much true of me

4. I enjoy helping others learn.		
Not very true of me	Somewhat true of me	Very much true of me

5. I like to share my expertise with my colleagues.		
Not very true of me	Somewhat true of me	Very much true of me

6. I have a particular area/problem/issue/idea that I would love to research and understand more fully.		
Not very true of me	Somewhat true of me	Very much true of me

7. I would like to develop my organization skills.		
Not very true of me	Somewhat true of me	Very much true of me

8. I want to learn how to design and develop presentations and training sessions.		
Not very true of me	Somewhat true of me	Very much true of me

HOW DOES IT BENEFIT THE LEARNER?

From developing and presenting brown-bag sessions or other short presentations, learners gain:

- Opportunities to practice preparing for and presenting a short presentation or workshop.
- Deeper understanding and knowledge about a topic of interest.
- Greater visibility in the organization.
- Reputation as an internal expert.
- A wider network of organizational contacts.
- Opportunities to practice for external presentations with a friendly audience of peers.

HOW DOES IT BENEFIT THE ORGANIZATION?

By engaging employees in the development and presentation of brown-bag sessions or other short presentations, the organization receives:

- Learning sessions to staff participants for no cost.
- Development opportunities to presenting staff for no cost.
- Collaborative knowledge management opportunities.
- Cross-training opportunities.
- Shared problem resolution strategies across teams/ departments.
- Enhanced internal expertise and depth of understanding of organization-specific areas of focus such as products and services, internal systems, or operational procedures.
- Increased employee engagement.
- Improved ability to reward/recognize high-performing employees (because publicly acknowledging them as experts and giving them the opportunity to present on their areas of expertise is a way to recognize their contributions and competence).

WHAT COMPETENCIES AND SKILLS CAN IT DEVELOP?

Designing, developing, and delivering a short training session or presentation can help develop several competencies, such as:

- Presentation skills.
- Project management or organization skills—by managing the project of design/development/scheduling the brown-bag session.
- Teamwork and collaboration—if the brown-bag is a team effort and the employee must collaborate with others to design, develop, and/or deliver it.
- Organization skills—in designing and developing a logical, well-organized presentation that is easy to follow.

Of course, the learners who attend the brown-bag session or presentation can also develop myriad competencies, skills, or knowledge based on the limitless list of possible topics that such a presentation or learning event can cover.

HOW DOES IT WORK?

How to Prepare

Organizations can institute a formal program with multiple offerings and speakers on a regular schedule (such as quarterly or monthly). However, it is possible to begin a grassroots approach or a pilot whereby the program is built one session at a time and gains momentum as it progresses. There isn't really a wrong way to do it, although there will be more preparation steps required for multi-session programs than for one-off sessions. First, answer these questions:

- What are the desired outcomes for this program?
- What measures will be used to assess the presenter's, session's, or program's progress and success?
- What might you or your organization need to do to ensure that this kind of investment of employee time and effort has valuable returns?

- What supplies are needed? What other resources are required?
- How will you or the presenter record and report an account of the development results?
- How will you celebrate progress and goal achievement?

Ways to Track Progress and Results

Employees who design, develop, and deliver presentations or brown-bag learning sessions can be evaluated in several different areas:

- delivery style
- organization
- program administration (how well they managed the registration, location setup, participant sign-in, and so on)
- content quality
- appropriateness for the audience.

Effectiveness of learning programs, whether one-hour brown-bag or multiday certification programs, are traditionally measured using Kirkpatrick's four levels of training evaluation (Kirkpatrick Partners, 2011):

Level 1: Reaction. To what degree did participants react favorably to the training? Ask participants to complete an evaluation survey after the session.

Level 2: Learning. To what degree did participants gain the intended knowledge, skills, attitudes, confidence, and commitment as a result of participating in the session? Test participants' knowledge or ability to perform a skill or behavior before and again after the session and measure the change.

Level 3: Behavior. To what degree do participants apply what they learned during the session when they are back on the job? Ask participants or their supervisors to assess their performance at a later point. Has their competency or skill level improved?

Level 4: Results (ROI). To what degree do targeted outcomes occur as a result of the brown-bag session and subsequent reinforcement? This is the most complex measure of all, and it may be more than what is necessary for a one-hour brown-bag lunch. For more on this subject, see Basarab, Kirkpatrick, and Kirkpatrick (2011) and Phillips, Phillips, Hodges, and Hodges (2004).

Implementation Tips

Below are some key steps to plan, in a general order of logical progression. You will need to tailor them to your specific topic, audience, logistics/scheduling needs, speaker requirements and availability, and any other factors that may affect their order.

Identify potential topics for brown-bag sessions. Sometimes the topic will arise in conversations with employees about their development needs or areas of interest, or in discussion with managers about success stories or problem resolution situations. You can also survey future learners about topics of interest or ask via your intranet site or internal social networking vehicles. Finally, consider offering a suggestion box (physical or virtual) to collect ideas on an ongoing basis.

Identify potential speakers. Some speakers will self-identify as a result of your topic query efforts (a topic will interest them, or they have experience or expertise in a particular area). Others may be identified by their managers or supervisors as a result of development conversations with those employees or in the course of relaying the aforementioned success stories or problem/solution situations.

Schedule the brown-bag session(s). Take into account venue and speaker availability and anticipated audience availability (for example, don't schedule brown-bag sessions in an accounting firm during tax season because people usually can't pull away from their desks to attend). For multi-session series, also consider frequency and spacing of the sessions—a predictable schedule of evenly distributed and regularly recurring sessions is more appealing than haphazardly scheduled brown-bag sessions with no apparent pattern of recurrence.

Advertise the session(s). Widely communicate the topic, speaker, session description, and learning objectives to get interest and encourage attendance. Beware of using the trademarked term *Lunch and Learn!* For more on the subject, see Miller and Shih (2010) and Reed Business Information (2011).

Register participants (optional). In some cases, you may want to encourage participants to register in advance. Doing this will help you know how many chairs to set out and how many handouts to print, as well as when the session becomes fully booked and you have to turn away any new participants or add them to a waiting list. Some organizations prefer to keep it simple and use a first-come, first-served policy for brown-bag sessions.

Evaluate and apply improvements based on feedback. Gather formal or informal feedback from participants (see the previous section on "Ways to Track Progress and Results" for more tips about evaluation) and use it to improve your next session(s).

Also, here are some tips for the presenter:

The presenter needs both knowledge and passion. The most effective learning events and presentations are the ones in which the speaker is both knowledgeable about the subject and passionate about sharing it with others.

Preparation is key. No matter how knowledgeable presenters are about their topic, providing a successful presentation or training session about it to others is not something they want to do off the cuff. Encourage presenters to take the time to prepare properly, so they can be organized, logical, and coherent. They will then be free to feel relaxed and in control, and participants will enjoy learning from them more as a result.

Practice, practice, practice. I know you've heard this before! Even though it's just a one- or two-hour session, even if participants are presenters' colleagues, and even though presenters are not being paid an honorarium, they will still want to be successful and proud of their work. Trying to wing it will not yield the best result—practicing a lot will.

Required Resources and Supports

Room—arrange to reserve a conference or training room in the building where the brown-bag session will be held. Consider reserving the space for an additional 15–30 minutes before and after the official start and end times of the session so you or the presenter can set up and break down your equipment and supplementary materials as well as greet participants and answer their questions.

Marketing/advertising—if no one knows about this session, all the presenter's preparation and work will have been in vain. Be sure to spread the word through all the appropriate internal communication channels. Some of these channels might include an employee newsletter, the organization's intranet site, training and development bulletins or learning management systems, breakroom and other bulletin boards, and so on.

Audiovisual equipment—if presenters are using a PowerPoint slide show or Prezi presentation, you will need to ensure that you provide them with an LCD projector and screen, as well as a computer and the proper cords. If presenters have a video or audio component in their session, be sure that there are properly functioning speakers hooked up and that the computer has the necessary program to run the file.

Printed handouts—the presenter may want to prepare some handouts so that the audience can follow along with key points, have materials to read further after the session, or be able to complete surveys, self-assessments, or any other exercises the presenter has designed. Arrange to have enough copies for the number of people expected to attend; it's a good idea to make five to 10 percent extra, just in case.

Supervisor and peer support—get presenters' supervisors onboard with the idea of developing their skills by presenting a brown-bag learning session. The supervisors will champion the presenters' session and support them with time and other resources. Presenters' peers (co-workers) should be recruited to support them so they may help with ideas for the presentation content or delivery, by spreading the word, and by acting as supportive audience members during the presentation.

Concerns/Downsides

Some potential concerns or objections that might arise about this kind of development approach include these:

Concern: People prefer to attend training workshops and presentations that are presented by professional presenters. They won't be interested in listening to an in-house presenter.

Overcome it: People like to listen to presenters who are interesting and interested in their own presentations. People enjoy presentations when the presenter is well prepared, organized, knowledgeable, and passionate. With the right topic and the right preparation, there is no reason for this concern to be true of this presentation.

Concern: Other employees will think that presenters are being boastful or showing off, or trying to get accolades, and will resent them.

Overcome it: Communicate the goal of the program widely and invite everyone to participate. Promote the benefits of peer-to-peer learning and help employees see it as an opportunity to collaborate, share, and learn "lessons from the front lines" or "from the trenches." Help presenters ensure that they take an inclusive, interactive, and collaborative approach and tone in the presentation to avoid inadvertently creating or fueling this misconception.

Concern: Other employees who were not selected to present during the brown-bag program may resent not having the opportunity and therefore not support the chosen presenter(s).

Overcome it: An equal-opportunity approach should help prevent this perception. Be careful to communicate the opportunity widely so that everyone who would want to present knows about it and has an equal chance to apply. If not, there may be valid concerns or perceptions of favoritism by those who missed out.

Concern: Presenter's fear of public speaking. Some people are great at their jobs, with clients, or one-on-one with peers, but don't feel comfortable about presenting to large audiences. The fear of public speaking is a common one, and it can pose a real barrier to successful presentations.

Overcome it: Support presenters by giving them ideas, tips, and coaching to prepare for presenting effectively. Don't throw them into a sink-or-swim situation where they don't feel competent or confident. And assure them that this is a great development opportunity for them, and that they will make strides toward improving their public speaking skills in a relatively low-stakes environment by working on this brown-bag session. Finally, you may suggest that presenters partner with a colleague who is more comfortable with presenting, so they could have a greater sense of comfort in a tag-team presentation. Additionally, the partner may take on the presenting aspects while the reluctant speaker focuses on the design and development of the session.

Concern: Some people who have a great story to tell or great skills to share may not be effective or compelling at presenting them. Their content may be good, but the session may not be successful because of a presentation skills deficiency.

Overcome it: Help deficient presenters by providing them with coaching on the art of training and presenting. Give them the opportunity to practice with someone who is a competent presenter and get some tips and feedback for improvement. And consider the co-presenter idea listed above as a way to ease presenters in without having all the pressure squarely on them.

RESOURCES

Basarab, D., D. Kirkpatrick, and J.D. Kirkpatrick. (2011). *Predictive Evaluation: Ensuring Training Delivers Business and Organizational Results.* San Francisco, CA: Berrett-Koehler Publishers.

Kirkpatrick Partners. (2011). *The Official Site of the Kirkpatrick Model.* Retrieved from http://www.kirkpatrickpartners.com/

Miller, A.M., and T. Shih. (2010, April 24). *Lunchtime Seminar or Invitation to a Trademark Infringement Lawsuit?* Retrieved from http://www.natlawreview.com/article/lunchtime-seminar-or-invitation-to-trademark-infringe ment-lawsuit

Phillips, J.J., P.P. Phillips, T. Hodges, and K. Hodges. (2004). *Make Training Evaluation Work.* Alexandria, VA: American Society for Training and Development.

Reed Business Information. (2011). *Lunch 'N Learn: Trademark Details.* Retrieved from http://media.zibb.com/trademark/lunch+'n+learn/29629606

Chapter 9

FUN AND GAMES: LEARNING VIA GAMES AND CONTESTS

WHAT IS IT?

Games and contests are special ways to attract and engage employees to learn, especially those who might not otherwise participate if the learning event is not mandatory. Games and contests often vividly demonstrate issues and the consequences of decisions. They are unusual, lively, and more stimulating than formal training classes or other communication campaigns. Employees' objectives for playing games and entering contests may be diversion or entertainment, a prize, or the possibility of winning. But you are able to also achieve the objective of developing them in the process.

Games entice people to think about different alternatives: root causes of problems; possible problem resolution ideas; benefits and uses of products, services, or systems; and a host of other business issues. They engage people interactively and are more effective than a matrix or another written description to show the consequences of actions. They enhance participation by giving people tangible, interesting, easy-to-relate-to activities rather than reams of reading material or workshops or meetings to attend. Brain research now shows that humans are naturally oriented toward the excitement and dopamine-releasing effects of around-the-corner surprises and potential, but uncertain, rewards. It's one of the reasons why investment bankers and high school students alike are addicted to flinging birds at objects in the smash-hit game Angry Birds while they ride on the subway to school or work. A testament to the popularity of games was when Angry Birds partnered with the movie *Rio* for its release: There were 10 million downloads in 10 days by people of different backgrounds, socioeconomic levels, ages, races, genders, and so on (Dignan, 2011).

Games and contests typically include:

- board games, for the tabletop or the computer
- card games
- computer simulation games or contests
- crossword puzzles or other word games
- games of chance, such as raffles
- games of skill, such as races, quiz shows, and Olympics-style contests
- essay, design, or poster contests.

Contests and games are unique methods for getting people's attention in subtle yet comprehensive ways that reach more employees and increase awareness, overall understanding, and even performance and skills about specific issues. The fun factor is important to acknowledge, because it breaks down barriers between various interest groups, generates goodwill for an issue or a product/service/system/process, and gives employees something interesting to look forward to. Indirectly, it also builds team and organizational engagement and cohesion.

For example, King's Family Restaurants, a 36-unit family-dining chain located in southern Pennsylvania, holds a "kitchen and service Olympics" contest every six months to focus employees on improving cleanliness, quality, and service in the restaurants. "We started the Olympics as we were revising our standards and putting together new menus," says Patti Evanosky, King's manager of training and development, in an interview for *Nation's Restaurant News* (Berta, 2011). Employees are judged on skills relevant to their specific roles: kitchen staff on culinary, food safety, and procedure thoroughness skills; servers on customer service quality; and all employees on how they serve one another. Teams and individuals can win various prizes and honors. They love it, and the company's positive and fun development approach achieves its objectives: clean stores and high-quality products and service. It also achieved a secondary benefit: The chain's average annual employee attrition dropped from 108 percent to 73 percent in three years in part due to this contest.

The Massachusetts Bay Transportation Authority (MBTA) created a board game called *On Track* to train its operators. Questions tested the operators' customer-service skills and knowledge of the MBTA system and its history. They ranged from how to get to the Children's Museum to what a bus driver should do if someone tried to board with a gorilla. Each question had three answers, ranked (using a dollar value) by degree of "correctness." Trainees got play money worth $10,000 if they said the gorilla should ride in the back of the bus and be restrained by its owner; they were docked $10,000 if they told the gorilla and its owner to get off the bus.

Similarly, the Pennsylvania Department of Transportation (DOT) created *Citizen Lane*, a board game used to train DOT employees on public involvement in project development, from preliminary design through construction. The one-hour game uses six sets of color-coded question cards for the phase of project development. The cards cover "incidents"—for example, what to do when 400 people show up at a room capable of holding 50—and "issues"—questions that challenge players to deal with potential major problems in a public involvement process. The "issues" cards require the six players to brainstorm together for an answer. The questions cover material included in the DOT's handbook on public involvement. Agency employees have been extremely enthusiastic about participating in workshops using *Citizen Lane*.

Such employee development efforts help staff understand what tools are useful in an engaging, fun, and easy-to-learn way (U.S. Department of Transportation, Federal Highway Administration, n.d.).

WHO SHOULD TRY IT?

This is a great development method for any type of organization and all types and levels of employees because challenging and fun games and contests have universal appeal. Games and contests are flexible in terms of type, where and when they can be used, staff time, and cost. Games are developed for varying levels of sophistication. Most employees are capable of developing or working with simple games, but complicated computer games or contests require specialized skills. Contests vary widely in complexity, depending on the nature of the project or plan and the issues to be addressed.

Certain kinds of games and contests may draw certain types of participants, though. For example, games that focus on artistic creativity may especially attract employees who enjoy being creative or are already artistically talented, and may deter those who don't see themselves as inherently creative. Contests that require specialized technical skills or knowledge may attract seasoned and expert employees and deter novices or new hires.

HOW DOES IT BENEFIT THE LEARNER?

Learners gain:
- new knowledge or skills in a fun and challenging way
- greater job satisfaction
- increased positive feelings of connection and engagement toward the organization
- divergence from everyday routine
- increased creative ideas and a new perspective on work issues
- interaction with peers that can foster team-building and enhanced cross-functional relationships.

HOW DOES IT BENEFIT THE ORGANIZATION?

Organizations can:
- Expand problem-solving resources.
- Leverage existing employees to generate new solutions and ideas outside their immediate job roles.

- Gain new insights into current practices and processes.
- Solve difficult business challenges.
- Enhance engagement and retention.
- Develop a sense of goodwill and commitment with employees.
- Develop employees' skills, knowledge, and abilities with little or no financial ramifications.
- Develop team and organizational cohesion.
- Create a positive and fun work environment.

WHAT COMPETENCIES AND SKILLS CAN IT DEVELOP?

Employees who engage in games or contests can develop multiple competencies depending on the subject matter and the type of game or contest, so here are a few of the most logical ones for your consideration:

- Interpersonal skills—when participating in a game or a contest, employees can work on considering and responding appropriately to the needs, feelings, and capabilities of different people in different situations. They can work on staying tactful and respectful instead of being overly competitive and using unfair game-play tactics.
- Influencing and negotiating—sometimes a game or contest calls on employees to get a team together or to gather funds or support from as many people as possible, which helps them develop their ability to persuade others, to build consensus, and to facilitate win-win situations.
- Creativity and innovation—many games and contests push employees to be creative and apply innovative solutions. In fact, some contests and games make creativity their main objective.
- Problem solving—if the game or contest calls on participants to identify and solve a problem, then it provides a great vehicle for developing the problem-solving competency.

145

HOW DOES IT WORK?

How to Prepare

To help prepare for using games and contests for development, answer the following questions:

- What are the desired outcomes for using these development tools?
- What measures will be used to assess the learner's progress and success?
- What might you or your organization need to do to ensure that this kind of investment of employee time and effort is well spent?
- How will you or your organization ensure that you communicate the purpose and desired outcomes of this type of learning?
- What support is needed? What resources are required?
- How will the learner record and report an account of learning and accomplishments?
- How will you celebrate progress and goal achievement?

Ways to Track Progress and Results

Depending on the nature of the contest or game and the competencies that each employee is working on developing, different measures will emerge as appropriate.

- If employees are working on developing interpersonal skills, they could journal about their interactions with others and describe the challenges that they experience during the game or contest. They could reflect on how they handle different challenges and draw insights about their results.

- If employees are working on developing their influencing skills, they could quantify the number of signatures they obtain on a petition or the monetary total of funds they raise.

- If the game or contest is focused on developing particular technical knowledge or skills, then you could consider how well employees fared in the game or contest as a measure of their ability to use the concepts or skills.

- Other ideas:

_____

_____

_____

_____

_____

Implementation Tips

Make it about battling boredom and anxiety: Make learning fun! Activities that rise above boredom but stop short of creating anxiety are the ones that really engage our interests and "hook us in" to a game. The idea is explained well by Hungarian psychologist Mihály Csíkszentmihályi (1990) in his concept of the state of flow. When we are in flow, we experience a loss of time perception and a suspension of our sense of self. We are totally immersed in our activity and in working toward mastery of it. And we enjoy this experience of being challenged continuously to push our skills just beyond our current abilities without feeling overwhelmed by a sense of incompetence (see Figure 9-1). Aaron Dignan, in his 2011 book *Game Frame*, explains how this idea meshes well with why humans

Figure 9-1 ■ Flow Diagram

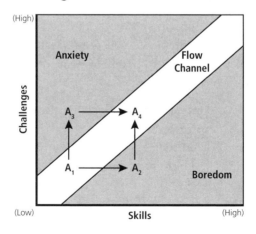

Source: Csíkszentmihályi (1990).

actively seek and welcome the challenge of games. "A lack of flow is the mind-numbing status quo experienced by too many white- and blue-collar workers," says Dignan. "Do I feel like I am getting better and better every day at my job, or am I feeling like my job is stagnating because I've mastered all the techniques and I'm sitting here wondering what to do next?"

Make it relevant and strategic. People need to understand how the game or contest relates to their work and how it supports the organization's strategic goals. The better this alignment, the less the perception that it's frivolous, and the more commitment and effort you will see from them.

Plan, design, and develop first. There is a bias for action and the allure of kicking off the excitement that can motivate us to launch a contest or game too quickly. In fact, the games that are the most interesting and engaging often take tremendous design expertise and advanced planning and development on the front end, even if they seem simple to the end user. Either develop this expertise in-house or outsource it to a consultant. Alternatively, use the resources mentioned in this chapter to approach this development method in a self-directed way. But don't cut short this important step in the process, because it will have a huge impact on the end results in terms of user clarity, participation, and enjoyment.

Simplify. Albert Einstein said it best: "Make everything as simple as possible, but not simpler." You need specificity so people know how to play. But don't overcomplicate it, or they will tune out or get discouraged.

Define goals, rules, and expectations. Participants must know the goal of the game or contest, the rules of participation, and the expectations you and their supervisors, as well as senior leadership, have for their level of commitment, amount of participation, and development outcomes.

Short is better than long. Generally, people will drop out more if your game or contest lasts longer than they care to participate, which is difficult to predict in the first place. So as a general rule of thumb, err on the side of making your game or contest have a quicker ending date and a faster pace if you want to maximize participation and minimize attrition.

Market, market, market. Unlike in the film *Field of Dreams* ("if you build it, he will come"), if you build a cool game or contest, but you don't tell employees about it, they will not necessarily sign up, show up, or play! Develop enticing marketing materials and communicate the "who, what, where, when, and why" of your game or contest to all the target audience members, early and often.

Evaluate and tweak. You don't have to have it perfect from the get-go. Start when you think it's good enough. Then monitor your game or contest and make course corrections. Also note lessons learned that can improve the next game or contest.

Required Resources and Supports

Game or contest design expertise. Use books and other self-directed learning resources, such as *The Book of Road-Tested Activities* (Biech, 2011), *The Big Book of Leadership Games* (Deming and Deming, 2004), and *Games That Teach* (Sugar, 1998). Or hire a game designer if this is a learning method you plan to employ regularly. Or, consider hiring a consultant to help you get ready.

Equipment, technology, and media resources. Depending on the kind of game or contest you plan to offer, you may need some technology tools or audiovisual equipment to run it. Ensure that you have all the necessary equipment before launching into game mode.

Tokens, boards, cards, and other supplies. Some games are played with game boards, playing cards, or other tools. Whatever supplies the game design calls for, be sure to have sufficient amounts to cover all the expected players, including some overage just in case.

Marketing and advertising materials. Design enticing marketing materials. You may need to have them printed and disseminated across various locations in time for your communication campaign, so plan ahead.

Prizes. Even though some people play games and enter contests for the sheer pleasure of participating or the accomplishment of the goal, many if not most will be lured in by the promise of cash and prizes. Think about ways to have multiple prize categories available and create as many winners as possible. And make the prizes as enticing and creative as you can. If money is no object, then of course throw lots of expensive prizes into the mix. But if your budget is tight, you can still come up with creative prizes that people find valuable and that carry very little or no monetary expenditure requirements.

Concerns/Downsides

Some of the opponents of this kind of development activity have voiced these concerns:

Concern: Games and contests do not interest everyone. Certain employees might resent their use or interpret playing games as trivializing the issues, as talking down to them, as a frivolous activity, or even as a waste of time and resources.

Overcome it: Avoid this perception by making sure the game relates clearly to the situation at hand and that the goals of using it are explained up front. Avoid forcing people to play; you may try to convince them and show them the benefits, of course, but don't make playing mandatory if at all preventable. Well-designed games are likely to hold people's interest better and longer than poorly designed ones.

Concern: Games and contests create happy winners and sore losers. Employees who lose may become discouraged, upset, or disengaged. They may doubt their ability to succeed and give up.

Overcome it: While everyone must remember good "gamesmanship" behaviors, it will be important to keep a finger on the pulse of sentiments and actively communicate with employees to discourage overly competitive and noncollaborative behavior. Remind those employees of the main goals of the game or contest and of the many benefits of sharing information with colleagues to increase the potential gains for everyone in the organization. Remind the "sore losers" about the main goals also, and encourage them to try again or to attempt to glean the ultimate development benefits regardless of the outcome.

Concern: Competitive employees may hoard information and keep the keys to their success in games and contests a secret. This lack of transparency can limit the organization's ability to reap the full potential of the game or contest.

Overcome it: When information sharing is key to success, organizations must ensure that employees get a fair chance to succeed and widely communicate the ultimate goal of the game. They must temper the communication about the contest from creating an overly competitive spirit that would then undermine its benefits, and discourage that kind of game play when and if certain employees display it.

Concern: What if my game falls flat? Employees might find the game or contest uninteresting or boring and not play or drop out.

Overcome it: Skillful design is important, as is clear communication about the basic point of an exercise. Even with best efforts, some games and contests may still have lackluster results, so you need to be prepared to mitigate the effects of boring games through lively discussion and follow-up.

Concern: Games and contests are too expensive to develop.

Overcome it: Designing good games and contests can require a significant time investment. Games are sometimes quite elaborate or expensive and require fancy hardware, software, or other equipment not normally available for other employee development efforts. Calculate the potential return on investment that can result from running a well-designed, successful game or contest to help sponsors understand the gains they can have. Alternatively, there are inexpensive and relatively simple contests or games available that you could repurpose just as successfully.

151

Search some of the websites (for example, www.thiagi.com) and books, such as *The Big Book of Conflict Resolution Games* (Scannell, 2010), that are suggested in the resources section of this chapter to get started.

CASE STUDY

When Michelle Moore was at IBM, the company had a sharing rally. The purpose was for each team, mostly marketing or service (which was her department), to improve a process. Michelle's team gathered and analyzed data and suggested a more straightforward way for customer engineers (CEs) to receive training for the products they fixed.

The current process at that time involved CEs going to training without requesting it or being told how it would benefit them. It was like "being told you were being sent to training for six weeks on something you never heard of." Instead, Michelle's team proposed that the CEs receive the training they needed based on their client install base, which would empower the CEs to choose the training they needed.

Michelle's team came in second place, which was a "big deal because we were not one of those polished marketing teams that was well versed in these skills already." Michelle says about her learning experience that "although I didn't realize it at the time, I learned a lot: how to gather data of all kinds; how to put it together to come to a conclusion; some presentation skills; and of course more about the Six Sigma methodology, which was the battle cry that year." Why didn't she realize that she was learning? Because she was focused on participating in a contest, having fun, collaborating with her team, and winning.

And the company was able to improve an inefficient process. A win–win–win!

RESOURCES

Berta, D. (2011, August 26). Restaurant Companies Boost Employee Morale With Contests, Games. *Nation's Restaurant News.* Retrieved from http://findarticles.com/p/articles/mi_m3190/is_26_38/ai_ n6095385/

Biech, E. (2008). *Trainer's Warehouse Book of Games: Fun and Energizing Ways to Enhance Learning.* San Francisco: Pfeiffer.

Biech, E. (2011). *The Book of Road-Tested Activities (Essential Tools Resource).* San Francisco: Wiley.

BlogTalkRadio.com. (2011, May 24). *Aaron Dignan on Why the Future of Work Is Play.* Retrieved from http://www.blogtalkradio.com/ creativityinplay/2011/05/24/aaron-dignan-on-why-the-future-of-work-is-play

Carlaw, P. (2007). *The Big Book of Customer Service Training Games: Quick, Fun Activities for All Customer Facing Employees.* New York: McGraw-Hill.

Carlaw, P., and V. Deming. (1999). *The Big Book of Sales Games: Quick, Fun Activities for Improving Selling Skills or Livening Up a Sales Meeting.* New York: McGraw-Hill.

Csíkszentmihályi, M. (1990). *Flow: The Psychology of Optimal Experience.* New York: Harper and Row.

Deming, V., and K. Deming. (2004). *The Big Book of Leadership Games: Quick, Fun Activities to Improve Communication, Increase Productivity, and Bring Out the Best in Employees.* New York: McGraw-Hill.

Dignan, A. (2011). *Game Frame.* New York: Free Press.

Hernandez, C. (2010, May 22). *How Employee Scavenger Hunts and Essay Contests Increase Customer Satisfaction.* Retrieved from http://www .smartplanet.com/blog/pure-genius/how-employee-scavenger-hunts-and-essay-contests-increase-customer-satisfaction/2787

Lomas, N. (2011, March 29). *Bored Staff? Gamification Could Change All That.* Retrieved from http://www.silicon.com/management/hr /2011/03/29/bored-staff-gamification-could-change-all-that-39747216/2/

Scannell, M. (2010). *The Big Book of Conflict Resolution Games: Quick, Effective Activities to Improve Communication, Trust and Collaboration.* New York: McGraw-Hill.

Sugar, S. (1998). *Games That Teach: Experiential Activities for Reinforcing Training.* San Francisco: Wiley.

Thiagi Group. (n.d.). *We Do Training.* Retrieved from www.thiagi.com

University of Windsor, Odette School of Business. (2011). *Employee Contests Don't Always Get Desired Results, Visiting Alumna Says.* Retrieved from http://business.uwindsor.ca/employee-contests-don%E2% 80%99t-always-get-desired-results-visiting-alumna-says

U.S. Department of Transportation, Federal Highway Administration. (n.d.). *Public Involvement Techniques for Transportation Decision-Making.* Retrieved from http://www.fhwa.dot.gov/reports/pittd/ games.htm

Vezina, K. (2011, August 17). Using Games to Get Employees Thinking: Organizations Can Make Productive Things Happen by Letting Their Workers Compete for Virtual Points. *Technology Review.* Retrieved from http://www.technologyreview.com/business/38191/

Chapter 10

DIGITAL STORYTELLING: LEARNING BY CREATING VIDEOS AND PODCASTS

WHAT IS IT?

All organizations have stories worth telling and local heroes worth knowing. The availability, the affordability, and the popularity of social learning technology have ripened the opportunities for capturing a vivid, engaging account of those heroes and their stories for harvesting. In chapter 12, we discuss how social learning provides a medium for learners to watch and listen to video and podcast content—that is, to be on the receiving end of the tools—to develop their competencies, knowledge, and skills. In this chapter, we'll explore how being on the other side of that equation—namely, creating the video- and audio-based social learning content—is a great learning opportunity as well. "Employees understand that when they capture themselves as an expert . . . they create a positive history . . . that positively reflects on themselves and their company" (Paolo Tosolini, in Weber, 2010).

Videocasting

A report from Cisco (2011) noted that 30 percent of Internet traffic is currently video. By 2013, 90 percent of Internet traffic will be video. Employees live in a world in which video is dominating their consumption of information, so why not invite more videocasts into the workplace and put them to good use? Whereas creating useful and relevant videos for the workplace used to be a costly and complicated endeavor, it can be done easily by anyone with a smart-phone, and media can be quickly and freely uploaded to a site such as YouTube for others to view within minutes. As consumers of video, we have become accustomed to watching low-tech, home-made clips and do not expect studio quality from our videocasts. Rather, we want them to be short, engaging, relevant, useful, and hopefully entertaining (although the latter is not a requirement).

For example, technicians working for Canada-based telecommu-nications company, TELUS, upload simple video images from their trucks and share them with their colleagues throughout the com-pany to find answers to questions that arise in the field (Bingham and Conner, 2010). Qualcomm, another telecom company based in California, captures and shares weekly employee stories from the trenches in a program called 52 Weeks. Employees submit, and the company promotes, memorable stories that showcase "a teachable moment with a learning lesson" that helps share information, trends, and attitudes and behaviors that reinforce the company's culture. While the stories are mostly text-based, this would be a great venue for using the videocasting medium to let employees tell their stories in short videos that could then be watched on the company's intranet site (Elkeles, 2010).

Podcasting

"Podcasting enables anytime, anywhere learning for a highly mo-bile workforce" (Sontakey, 2009). Podcasts are audio (but also video) recordings that can be downloaded and played on any MP3 or MP4 player such as iPod, iPhone, or Zune. Users can subscribe to RSS (originally RDF Site Summary, often dubbed Really Simple Syndication) feeds of podcasts in a podcast feed reader (Wikipedia, 2011b). Podcasts can also be distributed via a web-based system that contains a searchable catalogue of podcasts (Sontakey, 2009).

IBM uses podcasts to disseminate information across time zones to its global employee base to cut the costs of internal communica-tion and training. EMC supplements executive training by tooling the learners with preloaded iPods full of business book summaries. Financial services provider Capital One distributes iPods as standard equipment to employees enrolled in training courses to be used for listening to podcasts that support their classroom and online training (Hoglund, 2009). In the same vein, any organization can equip its employees with current, reliable, insider information that is relevant to their work and created by their peers. Recently it was reported that more than 90 million Americans drive alone to work every day—listening to something in their cars (Hoglund, 2009). Their options include music, news, talk radio, and audiobooks. So why not add the option of listening to podcasts they download that are uploaded by their peers at their office or at another office across the globe?

The Content Possibilities

There is a wide range of possible types of stories that lend themselves to this kind of medium. Here are a few ideas to get you started:

- Peers feature their peers' stories of success, lessons learned, problems solved, questions and challenges they want input about, gratitude, quandaries, and other "teachable moments."
- Employees interview or capture the stories of insider heroes, "rock stars," or celebrities—some employees become local legends because they're popular with clients, they're known for helping colleagues, or they have great ideas or solutions to common problems.
- Staff members interview or capture the story of VIPs (very important persons) within the company, such as top executives and business unit leaders.
- Podcasts and videocasts can feature how-to content about a product, service, system, tool, process, or shortcut, or any other useful information to help other employees do their jobs better.
- Employees can record stories and interviews of happy customers telling about their experiences with the organization or a specific employee, product, or service.

- Executives can share success stories or tips about how they deal with a particular work problem or challenge. At Beers and Cutler (now part of Baker Tilly), a U.S.-based accounting firm, executives shared their "elevator speech" with associates via recorded podcasts.
- Employees' videos of company events, road shows, off-site meetings, training sessions, or customer presentations can help enhance organizational engagement, culture building, and team building.

The Technology

There are lots of options, and the number increases rapidly, daily, with the onslaught of new, cheaper, and better technology and vendors. Here are some examples of solution ideas at time of print:

Microsoft offers a Podcast-in-a-Box program to help get employees recording, sharing, and teaching their peers (Weber, 2010). The equipment it requires is Camtasia Studio, a Flip Video camera for video recording, or Samsung's products (recommended by Tosolini as the highest-quality recording for cheap) for podcasting. Microsoft invested in about 200 kits, for its 22,000 staff, that were used to create more than 2,000 podcasts in two years (Weber, 2010). Nice and Serious, a U.K.-based environmental and ethical film production company, lets organizations rent an employee-generated video (EGV) production kit on a weekly basis. The kit contains a Sony Bloggie HD video camera, a compact tripod, memory cards, and access to online tutorials for using the camera. The company then edits your footage into a short video (LinkedIn, 2011). Kontiki (2011) is a YouTube-like enterprise, as is Qumu (2010).

WHO SHOULD TRY IT?

Anyone can do it. Some employees may be more interested, more inclined to the technical or creative aspects of it, or more experienced than others and therefore have a lower barrier to entry than others. Organizations may find that by leveraging those employees who already have the equipment, the experience, or an intrinsic motivation to learn it, they can begin implementing the program quickly to create seed content. This content and activity will build momentum and interest. And with social learning being easily viral, the opportunity will create interest and motivation in others and lower inhibitions in the more novice employees who may consider giving this kind of learning a try.

The opportunity should definitely be available to employees of all levels of the organization's hierarchy, from frontline employees through executives, although at Microsoft, statistics showed that the vast number of employee-generated podcasts were created by employees as opposed to executives (see Figure 10-1; Tosolini in Weber, 2010).

Figure 10-1 ▪ Who Created More Podcasts at Microsoft?

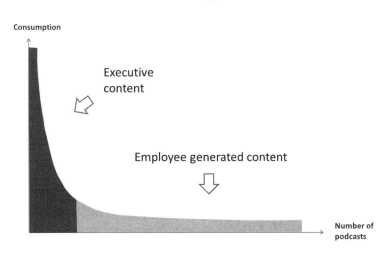

By far the best content will be the product of content creators who are interested in doing it and enjoy the experience.

Before they embark on a podcasting or videocasting learning adventure, encourage learners to assess their readiness for this kind of learning using Figure 10-2.

Figure 10-2 ■ Self-Assessment: Podcasting or Videocasting Readiness

Respond to the statements by placing an X along each spectrum.

1. I like to help develop other people by sharing key information with them.		
Not very true of me	Somewhat true of me	Very much true of me

2. I like to identify ideas, examples, people, or stories that other employees would find useful and interesting.		
Not very true of me	Somewhat true of me	Very much true of me

3. I want to develop my interviewing skills.		
Not very true of me	Somewhat true of me	Very much true of me

4. I enjoy helping others learn.		
Not very true of me	Somewhat true of me	Very much true of me

5. I like to learn from my colleagues and co-workers.		
Not very true of me	Somewhat true of me	Very much true of me

6. I have a particular area/problem/issue/idea that I would love to understand more fully by finding an internal expert to help me learn.		
Not very true of me	Somewhat true of me	Very much true of me

7. I would like to develop my project management and organization skills.		
Not very true of me	Somewhat true of me	Very much true of me

8. I want to learn how to design and develop podcasts or videos.		
Not very true of me	Somewhat true of me	Very much true of me

HOW DOES IT BENEFIT THE LEARNER?

Learners gain:

- opportunities to learn how to create and produce podcasts and/or videocasts
- faster, better understanding about a topic of interest
- greater visibility in the organization
- a wider network of organizational contacts
- opportunities to develop project management and organization skills
- access and connection to high-level executives and experts.

HOW DOES IT BENEFIT THE ORGANIZATION?

Organizations gain:

- Cost and time savings on employee development offerings. User-generated content is basically free. With no lengthy course development cycles, content gets to the field faster while it is most relevant.
- Increased employee knowledge around products, competitors, processes, and best practices.
- Enhanced capability of field staff to communicate just-in-time feedback to sales, product, and learning leadership (Hoglund, 2009).
- Greater distribution of control and ownership of learning content resulting in greater empowerment and better employee development options available compared to a limited-participation content creation model.
- Faster access to new information, and faster distribution throughout the enterprise.
- Collaborative knowledge management opportunities.
- Cross-training opportunities.
- Shared problem resolution strategies across teams/departments.
- Enhanced internal expertise and depth of understanding of organization-specific areas of focus such as products and services, internal systems, or operational procedures.
- Increased employee engagement.

WHAT COMPETENCIES AND SKILLS CAN IT DEVELOP?

The subject matter of the videocasts and podcasts can vary greatly and thus facilitate the development of a wide range of competencies. Some of the unique competencies that can be greatly developed in the employee who engages in this activity include:

- Creativity and innovation—planning and creating videocasts or podcasts requires employees to design and implement new programs and use creative thinking and innovation to make effective and useful media products.

- Partnering—employees can develop networks and build alliances across functions and boundaries when they set out to find subjects for their videocasts or podcasts, thereby developing the partnering competency.
- Oral communication—if employees want to improve their ability to facilitate an open exchange of ideas and foster an atmosphere of open communication, videocasts or podcasts could help. Employees could engage in a project to create videocasts or podcasts in which they facilitate panel discussions featuring divergent ideas and foster dialogue among the key speakers, for example.

HOW DOES IT WORK?

How to Prepare

Organizations can institute a formal podcasting or videocasting program with multiple offerings on a regular schedule (such as weekly, monthly, or quarterly). However, it is possible to begin a grassroots approach or a pilot whereby the program is built one segment at a time and gains momentum as it progresses. There isn't really a wrong way to do it, although there will be more preparation steps required for multi-session programs than for one-off segments. First, answer these preparation questions:

- What are the desired outcomes for this program?
- What measures will be used to assess the progress and success of the podcast/videocast producer, session, or program?
- What might you or your organization need to do to ensure that this kind of investment of employee time and effort has valuable returns?
- What supplies are needed? What other resources are required?
- How will you or the podcast/videocast producer record and report an account of the development result?
- How will you celebrate progress and goal achievement?

Ways to Track Progress and Results

Based on the competencies that employees have selected to target, here are some ideas about how to measure and track progress.

- If working to improve their creativity and innovation competency, employees could present their final products to be assessed for creativity by the manager. Another way to assess this indirectly is to track ratings or comments for the video or podcast via the social learning system it's posted on.
- When the goal is partnering development, employees may journal about their experiences interacting with different departments or roles and insights gleaned from those interactions about new ways to view the problem or issue at hand. You could also set a goal to feature a set list of departments or different perspectives and then measure whether employees achieved that goal.
- Other ideas:

_____

_____

_____

_____

_____

_____

Implementation Tips

Here are some suggestions that can help you make the most of this effort:

Think of the audience. Consider what internal stakeholders would benefit from seeing and hearing.

Just start. You don't have to have it all figured out at first. It's better if you just get started and tweak along the way.

Communicate. Share your goals and the purpose of this learning type, since it may be novel to many employees.

Provide examples. Promote the best examples of employee-generated video—people learn best by modeling after exemplars.

Start easy. Pick easy-to-use technologies—especially initially—to reduce fear of technology playing as a major barrier to entry.

Involve all levels. Give executives a direct link to employees and vice versa to ensure that all levels of the organization are visibly involved and contributing.

Celebrate! Acclaim wins and generate team spirit.

Create contingencies. Consider lending the equipment with strings attached. For example, Microsoft encouraged its employees to try podcasting by offering them a Podcast-in-a-Box kit including podcast or video recording equipment and required those who wanted to keep the gear to publish at least three podcasts per month. If not, the gear would be transferred to another interested employee.

Stay on it. This program needs to be actively managed. Some attrition will naturally occur. But if no one actively monitors, promotes, and coaches the program participants/learners to generate new content and engage in interaction with the audience, the program could become stale and lose credibility.

Required Resources and Supports

Video and podcasting equipment. While you definitely don't need a $100K camera or a full film crew, there are some pieces of equipment and software that are required to get this project off the ground. However, many organizations have experimented with using the most basic, low-tech tools like smartphones and simple camcorders to get started (see the British Airways case study at the end of this chapter for such an example). Another suggestion to make this effort truly low cost is to identify and invite employees who have this kind of equipment already to be the pioneers of this new program.

- **For video:** You will need a decent $600–$1,200 HD camera (such as the Sony Webbie HD or the Kodak Zi8) and video editing software (such as Final Cut or Pinnacle Studio). The iPhone 4's 720p HD camera and iMovie app might suit you fine. Affordable HD cameras are now widely available, and the market keeps changing, so do a search to identify the most current equipment options, prices, and user ratings. Careful lighting and a solid tripod can make the footage from any camera look great. The catch with lower-cost HD cameras will be in their limited audio quality and limited types of microphone inputs. To deal with this challenge, you could limit the videos you make for the web to nonsync sound. Alternatively, you could choose to invest in a system for recording sound separately (such as BeachTek's DXA-5D; Menicucci, 2010).

- **For podcasts:** The quality of your microphone has more of an effect on the overall quality of your recordings than any other device, so spend your money here if your budget is limited (try the Rode Podcaster Dynamic USB Mic or even the inexpensive Logitech ClearChat Comfort USB Headset). You'll also probably need some cables, a mic stand, and booms. You also need a good set of headphones for recording, so typical headphones and iPhone headsets may not be good enough (try Sony MDR7506 Professional Large Diaphragm Headphones or Audio-Technica ATH-M30 Professional Headphones). If you're using an XLR mic, you'll also need an audio interface to plug into your computer to translate the signal. You may choose to use a mixer instead. Podcasting software can run the gamut of prices and quality, and a program that you might like to try at first (for free!) is Audacity. Finally, you may also need streaming software like Wirecast. A comprehensive list is found at Hivelogic (2011). Check out the free podcasting equipment list from Jonathan Halls and Associates (2010)— it even has a shoestring option!

Hosting and sharing website. Either use your organization's intranet or social learning network (if applicable), or use one of the many video and podcast streaming, feed, and hosting websites widely available such as YouTube, Vimeo, Odeo, Libsyn, or Ourmedia.

Concerns/Downsides

Some of the opponents of this kind of development activity have voiced concerns. Some of them are similar to the concerns with social learning in general.

Concern: It's expensive to get all the equipment and software. It's not in my budget, and I don't think I can prove the return-on-investment (ROI) for this kind of expenditure.

Overcome it: It can be expensive if you choose the Rolls-Royce version of the systems and tools that are on the market, but you can also offer many of the benefits of video and podcasting to your organization for little to no up-front cost by using some of the widely available free and low-cost tools on the market and work within their existing parameters and constraints. Also, if you leverage existing equipment that may already be in the hands of some employees (they already own it and can be your early adapters and pilot participants), you can build slowly and gain momentum. You can start small and cheap and then make a stronger case for ROI once the program is in place and you can quantify results.

Concern: Users may generate offensive or irrelevant videos or podcasts that may cause a potential misuse of these learning vehicles or possibly violate the security policy.

Overcome it: You can avoid this problem by adding a moderation layer and only publish content after you (or select moderators) review and approve it.

Concern: Some employees will enjoy these learning activities so much they will spend a disproportionately large amount of time on them. This will prevent them from meeting their performance goals and job priorities.

Overcome it: Just like any other potential derailment and distraction, this too must be one that is actively monitored and managed by the employee's supervisor. For great performance to take place, employees must know what their managers expect of them, know how their performance will be measured, and have ongoing feedback conversations to keep them on track. Active and effective ongoing performance management (which is assumed as the standard with or without video and podcasting in place) allows the organization, and its employees, to stay effective, productive, and successful.

Concern: No benchmarks or performance measurements exist for these learning activities. They do not lend themselves to tracking and measuring employee learning like traditional instructor-led and e-learning platforms do.

Overcome it: While you can't measure learning directly, there are ways you can measure it indirectly. When employees add comments to videos and podcasts, you could qualitatively assess the knowledge they gained and their level of expertise. Furthermore, you could assess users through community polls and surveys. Additionally, users can rate content (using the stars or "thumbs-up" ratings embedded in the hosting systems), which can further indicate interest and preferences and help assess the quality of the online experts.

Concern: Videos are for fun, not for real knowledge transfer or serious business.

Overcome it: "Images combined into a narrative are a major component of effective communication and therefore appropriate for business; and the power to instruct is inherent in video" (Bingham and Conner, 2010).

Concern: Technology—we don't have the appropriate tools or video/podcast sharing system in place.

Overcome it: "It doesn't have to be slick, polished, or professional. It just has to be made available. That's the first step" (Pontefract, 2011).

CASE STUDIES

British Airways Video Contest

Airline British Airways (BA) decided to encourage innovative learning by launching a video competition called "Winning Ways in the Workplace" in May 2011. The company collaborated with e-learning specialist BrightWave and video production partner Nice Media to open this contest to all BA employees. The challenge? Employees were invited to create a short (maximum two minutes) video on a smartphone or camcorder to demonstrate a technique, a shortcut, or an attitude that helps them do their job more effectively.

The idea behind the challenge was to show how user-generated learning content allows all employees to capture and share knowledge. This complements more formal workplace learning, as well as contributes to a positive learning culture and improved performance. This particular story could also complement our chapter on games and contests (chapter 9).

Howrey Ghost Stories

To foster interpersonal skills such as teamwork, communication, and empathy among members of a law firm's trial team, Howrey created a program called "Howrey Ghost Stories." Filming case studies acted out by staff members, Howrey Ghost Stories lets team members explore "how the dynamics among the members of a typical client team can affect a case." With the exception of one professional actor, all roles are played by Howrey lawyers and depict team dynamics with scripted segments interspersed with unscripted interviews of characters about their own motivations and those of other team members in the story. The firm released one episode per week on its intranet site, asking viewers to vote on their favorite character, suggest alternative actions for key junctions in the team's interpersonal interactions, and drill deeper into particular issues by plugging into additional training modules (Bock and Berman, 2011).

RESOURCES

Bavosa, M. (2011, April 6). *101 Online Video Stats to Make Your Eyes Glaze Over*. Retrieved from http://engage.tmgcustommedia.com /2011/04/101-online-video-stats-to-make-your-eyes-glaze-over/

Bingham, T., and M. Conner. (2010). *The New Social Learning: A Guide to Transforming Organizations Through Social Media*. Alexandria, VA: American Society for Training and Development and San Francisco: Berrett-Koehler.

Black, H. (2010, June 4). *4 Tips for Producing Quality Web Videos*. Retrieved from http://mashable.com/2010/06/04/producing-quality-web-videos/

Bock, H., and L. Berman. (2011, February). Learning and Billable Hours— Can They Get Along? *T+D*. Available from http://www.astd.org/TD/ Archives/2011/TOC/1102FebTOC.htm

Bozarth, J. (2010). *Social Media for Trainers: Techniques for Enhancing and Extending Learning (Essential Tools Resource)*. San Francisco, CA: Pfeiffer.

Cisco. (2011, June 1). *Cisco Visual Networking Index: Forecast and Methodology, 2010–2015*. Retrieved from http://www.cisco.com/en/US /solutions/collateral/ns341/ns525/ns537/ns705/ns827/white _paper_c11-481360_ns827_Networking_Solutions_White_Paper.html

Elkeles, T. (2010, March). In Practice: Storytelling Drives Knowledge and Information Sharing Across Qualcomm. *Chief Learning Officer*, p. 23.

Elliott, A.-M. (2010, June 3). *HOW TO: Make a Great How-To Video*. Retrieved from http://mashable.com/2010/06/03/how-to-make-how-to-video/

Hivelogic. (2011, April 8). *Podcasting Equipment Guide*. Retrieved from http://hivelogic.com/articles/podcasting-equipment-software-guide-2011/

Hoglund, T. (2009). *Learning 2.0: Driving High Performance With New Strategies, Tools, and a Broader Mission*. Retrieved from http://www .accenture.com/SiteCollectionDocuments/PDF/ACC_4165 _learning_010609_2.pdf

The Huffington Post. (2011, June 8). *Social Media Statistics 2011: Amazing Facts About Internet Use*. Retrieved from http://www.huffington post.com/2011/06/08/social-media-statistics-2011_n_873116.html

Islam, K.A. (2007). *Podcasting 101 for Training and Development: Challenges, Opportunities, and Solutions*. San Francisco, CA: Pfeiffer.

JonathanHalls.net. (2011). *Articles and Tips to Improve Your Management; Articles and Tips for Creating New Media Content*. Retrieved from http://jonathanhalls.net/

Jonathan Halls and Associates. (2010). *Podcasting Equipment*. Retrieved from http://jonathanhalls.com/resources/gw-audio-lab/podcasting-equipment/

Kontiki. (2011). *Enterprise Video Communications*. Retrieved January 6, 2012, from http://www.kontiki.com

LinkedIn. (2011). *Employee Generated Videos*. Retrieved from http://www.linkedin.com/company/nice-and-serious/employee-generated-videos-109043/product

Meister, J.C., and K. Willyerd. (2010). *The 2020 Workplace: How Innovative Companies Attract, Develop, and Keep Tomorrow's Employees Today*. New York, New York: HarperBusiness.

Menicucci, H. (2010, June 18). *6 Tips For Experimenting with Web Video*. Retrieved from http://mashable.com/2010/06/18/tips-for-web-video/

Pontefract, D. (2011, May 16). *Why Don't You Have an Internal YouTube Video Sharing Service?* Retrieved from http://www.danpontefract.com/?p=965

Qumu. (2010). *What Is Enterprise Video? Live Webcasts, Employee Generated Content, Video Portals, and More*. Retrieved from http://www.youtube.com/watch?v=pIXo62TYzZU

Sontakey, A. (2009). Compress Your Learning Curve: Improve Enterprise Learning Through Collaboration and Knowledge Sharing. *Infosys SET-Labs Briefings* 7(3). Retrieved from http://www.infosys.com/infosys-labs/publications/setlabs-briefings/Pages/compress-your-learning-curve.aspx

Training Magazine Network. (n.d.). *TrainingPayback*. Available from http://www.trainingmagnetwork.com/discussions/show/2661

Training Press Releases. (2011, May 16). *British Airways "Winning Ways" Workplace Video Challenge*. Retrieved from http://www.trainingpressreleases.com/newsstory.asp?NewsID=6361

Weber, B. (2010, April 27). *How to Get Employee Generated Content. . . .* Retrieved from http://visuallounge.techsmith.com/2010/04/how_to_get_employee_generated.html

Wikipedia. (2011a). *List of Podcatchers*. Retrieved from http://en.wikipedia.org/wiki/List_of_podcatchers

Wikipedia. (2011b). *RSS*. Retrieved from http://en.wikipedia.org/wiki/RSS

Chapter 11

ZONING OUT: LEARNING THROUGH INNOVATION/ CREATIVITY ZONES

WHAT IS IT?

What if you could develop skills you could use on the job by actually not doing your job for a bit? This is a revolutionary idea that has been slowly taking hold in some of the more innovative and creative companies, and you should consider giving it a try at your organization. Companies such as Google have gained some of the most groundbreaking creative ideas and innovations by allowing their employees to take time to work on something that doesn't fall within the parameters of their day-to-day job for a specific amount of time. This timeframe—a dedicated "Innovation/Creativity Zone"—is time employees can spend chasing down an idea, doing an experiment, or conducting research. The only requirement is that the employees report back what they have accomplished during that dedicated chunk of time away from work.

Author Daniel Pink wrote about this concept in his 2010 book, *Drive: The Surprising Truth About What Motivates Us*. Pink describes how once a quarter, on a Thursday afternoon, Australian software company Atlassian allows its developers to work on anything they want to, any way they want to, and with whomever they wish. The only requirement Atlassian imposes on this dedicated zone time is that employees must show what they've created to the rest of the company at a high-energy meeting 24 hours later (which also involves cake and other fun treats). They call these sessions

"FedEx Days" because people have to deliver something overnight. The results? FedEx Days have produced a slew of fixes for existing software as well as ideas for new products that might not have emerged otherwise.

Google, the oft-praised employer of choice, does something similar; the company calls it "20 percent time." Google's engineers are encouraged to take 20 percent of their work time to work on something company-related that interests them personally. Instead of a specific day of the quarter where everyone takes this special time together, however, here employees are encouraged to take the time when they want to. So if you think of a great idea, and you're managing your schedule so that you can meet your regular job deadlines and requirements, you take the time when the creative spirit strikes you and explore your idea. Fifty percent of Google's innovative products have come from 20 percent time!

According to Bharat Mediratta (2007), a Google engineer, "People work better when they're involved in something they're passionate about, and many cool technologies have their origins in 20 percent time, including Gmail, Google News, and even the Google shuttle buses that bring people to work at the company's headquarters in Mountain View, California."

3M has probably pioneered this concept—since the 1930s and 1940s, 3M has had a similar initiative, called "15 percent culture," to encourage technical employees to spend 15 percent of their time on projects of their own choosing and initiative. We can thank this 15 percent culture for Post-It® notes!

Social media icon Twitter has incorporated Hack Week, during which Twitter employees develop solutions and ideas for services that are separate from their day-to-day jobs. According to Twitter's blog post on it, "There aren't many rules—basically we'll work in small teams and share our projects with the company at the end of the week. What will happen with each project will be determined once it's complete. Some may ship immediately, others may be added to the roadmap and built out in the future, and the remainder may serve as creative inspiration" (Twitter Engineering, 2010). Similarly, Facebook and Foursquare have incorporated the practice of "Hackathons"—daylong events that lead to the development of new apps, products, and services. For example, four Facebook employees developed a working demo of Facebook's 'Timeline' in an all-night hackathon in 2010 (Constine 2012).

The good news is that you don't have to have a monthly week-long time-out, 15 percent time, 20 percent time, or any other set amount of time to benefit from such a focused zone time to develop your employees' skills and interests. Even the smallest amount of time in a recurring pattern (such as first thing each morning for 30 minutes, or every Friday from 10 a.m. to 12 p.m., or the last Friday of each month, and so on) could bring learners development benefits.

WHO SHOULD TRY IT?

While any employee can benefit and use this kind of focused time to work on a side project, the ones who will likely benefit the most are employees who are achievement oriented, interested in being creative, and passionate about some aspect of the organization's current or possible future work. And unless the special zone is shared and done as a group activity (as during Atlassian's FedEx Days), employees who pursue this kind of time on their own may need to be able to show self-directedness and an ability to manage time and productivity effectively. This method could require more resources and structure, but in reality, this method can be successfully implemented with very little of either.

Employees who are interested in pursuing this type of development approach should complete the assessment in Figure 11-1 to see if this is a good fit for their needs.

HOW DOES IT BENEFIT THE LEARNER?

Innovation/creativity zones allow learners to:
- Develop creativity on the job.
- Learn new skills and competencies while working productively to benefit the organization.

- Achieve greater sense of empowerment over their own development.
- Spend focused time thinking outside their own roles/job duties to fully tap underutilized strengths. This also leads to greater satisfaction in learners' own roles.
- Feel greater commitment of the organization to their development and growth.
- Positively affect other lines of service or business units.
- Potentially increase their organizational network of contacts.
- Produce and present an outcomes report to peers and leaders throughout the organization about the results.

Figure 11-1 ▪ Innovation/Creativity Zone Readiness

Respond to the statements by placing an X along each spectrum.

1. I enjoy thinking of creative new ideas.		
Not at all like me	A little like me	Very much like me

2. I am a self-directed worker—I can make and follow a plan on my own.		
Not at all like me	A little like me	Very much like me

3. I am results-oriented, always working to achieve a new goal.		
Not at all like me	A little like me	Very much like me

4. I feel passionate about the work that I do.		
Not at all like me	A little like me	Very much like me

5. I believe in the mission of my organization.		
Not at all like me	A little like me	Very much like me

6. I feel frustrated that I can't spend enough time on ideas during my workweek because of urgent deadlines and daily commitments.		
Not at all like me	A little like me	Very much like me

7. If I could just focus and concentrate in an uninterrupted fashion on an idea or a project, I could achieve breakthroughs in creating new solutions or developments.		
Not at all like me	A little like me	Very much like me

HOW DOES IT BENEFIT THE ORGANIZATION?

Innovation/creativity zones also benefit the organization, allowing it to:

- Expand problem-solving resources.
- Tap into a broader pool of talent without adding head count.
- Gain new insights into current practices, processes, and offerings.
- Develop new offerings using existing resources. Google claims that 50 percent of its new products or innovations in any given year are developed during 20 percent time.
- Solve difficult business challenges.
- Enhance engagement and retention of capable, high-achieving staff.
- Develop sense of goodwill and commitment with employees.
- Develop employees' skills, knowledge, and abilities with little or no financial ramifications.
- Reduce brain drain (attrition of top performers).

WHAT COMPETENCIES AND SKILLS CAN IT DEVELOP?

Lots of different competencies can be developed by this kind of activity. A few key examples include:

- Creativity and innovation—of course!
- Strategic thinking—thinking about innovation in the context of the business and competitive strategy in a global economy leads to innovative, out-of-the-box thinking and solutions to tough business problems.
- Team building—working with others on a zone project can help employees develop this competency, which calls for inspiring, motivating, and guiding others toward goal accomplishments.
- Oral communication—the final report about the results of the zone time can develop employees' abilities to present their ideas clearly and convincingly to individuals or groups.

HOW DOES IT WORK?

How to Prepare

In order to prepare before starting down this path, consider these key questions to help ensure that this development method is successful in practice:

- What are the desired outcomes for this activity or program?
- What measures will be used to assess the learner's progress and success?
- What might you or your organization need to do to ensure that this kind of investment of employee time and effort is well spent?
- How will you, the learner, or your organization ensure that you communicate the purpose and desired outcomes of this initiative/activity?
- What will you, the learner, or your organization do to protect the time from interruptions?
- What supplies are needed? What other resources are required?
- How will you, the learner, or the group support ongoing customer service coverage and maintain ongoing business processes and operations during this dedicated learning time? Can you arrange for people to pinch-hit for each other while in this dedicated zone?
- How will you, the learner, or the group record and report an account of progress and learning as well as accomplishments?
- How will learners celebrate progress and goal achievement?

Ways to Track Progress and Results

The main goal of the dedicated creativity/innovation zone is to get and stay focused and creative. And that's hard to measure. It's also hard to mandate a certain quantity or quality of outcome—that defeats the purpose. It's probably best to keep measures light on the short-term side of things, such as simply sharing the products of the zone time with others similar to Atlassian's FedEx Day report. This report is a type of measure—employees can't report anything if they didn't do anything, after all. Additionally, requiring a report as a deliverable creates external performance pressure, since we naturally don't want to be seen as slackers to our boss or colleagues.

What other measures can you use?

_____

_____

_____

_____

_____

Implementation Tips

Inspire a vision. You will need to inspire others to support and even follow you to implement this type of development activity. Therefore, you really need to be clear on your own vision of success for this idea and be able to communicate it to others in a way that rallies them around it. Your desired outcomes or goal definitions will come in handy.

Give it time. This is the kind of development activity that is easy to start on a whim and on a shoestring, especially if you start small and implement it incrementally. Yet I would suggest you give it time so that it can take hold and grow strong roots. So try a "FedEx Half-Day" at first, or 10 percent time. Find your organization's appropriate rhythm to identify the most appropriate space/time for this kind of learning, and be willing to experiment.

Begin small. Consider starting with just a few employees or a small group, rather than everyone. You can call it a pilot to help sell people on the idea without overwhelming them. Also, emphasize that you would like to try it for a test period, not forever. This will allow you to make tweaks or to surrender altogether if it doesn't work and minimizes the level of commitment from those who are suspicious or apprehensive.

Give it support. You have to provide scaffolding or a support system to prop up the initiative when it's new and not yet mature and understood well by all. Think about ways that can help create advocacy, support, and enthusiasm for your idea. Also think about who you can recruit to help promote and uphold the cause. The more support in your scaffolding, the better your chance of success.

Be patient. Know that success rarely comes overnight, and any good practice takes time to form. Don't expect miracles, and be patient and willing in your experimentation to accept small wins at first with the belief that big wins will come eventually. Like a kid who abandons her piano lessons because she is not impressed with her ability to play only the three-note "Little Indian" tune when she envisioned Mozart rolling off her fingertips, don't make a mistake of judging too harshly what is a momentum-building nascent idea. Help others be patient, too.

Show commitment and grit. Have the commitment, discipline, and grit to withstand the inevitable false starts and bumps in the road. It takes time for this practice to take hold and begin bearing fruit. While experimenting, hold on to your ideas and don't dismiss the process you created too quickly just because it didn't work perfectly the first time.

Be trusting and trustworthy. Good relationships and mutual trust, as well as a sense of mutual collegial accountability, are at the core of this practice, especially if applied to groups rather than on an individual level. Organizations with low trust are probably not going to agree to give employees this much autonomy in the first place, and they will experience difficulty if they do because they don't believe that people will keep their word and protect their investment.

Required Resources and Supports

Time—the time commitment required depends on how you approach the zone. An all-hands or whole-team effort will require more time and collaborative preparation than an individual independently working on a 15- or 20-percent project.

Not a lot of money—this development method will cost very little money, if any, except for the cost of the time taken away from other work duties and spent in the zone activities, if accomplished independently by individuals. If you make it a team effort, there may be costs for a venue, refreshments, and supplies.

Support of peers and leaders—other employees may be called on to support the learners in the zone by covering for them if the employee takes some time away from their usual duties to focus on a zone project. It will be great if direct supervisors support the learners by allowing them to invest their time and energy in the zone work.

Organizational and infrastructure support—the more robust and structured the organization's support is for creativity/innovation zones, the more sustainable the practice will be. Organizational support can be demonstrated by creating a zone infrastructure that is scalable, strong, and tied to the organization's strategic goals, and that has a demonstrated commitment of and support from senior leadership. Some infrastructure supports include roll-out support, administration, implementation, technology, connection with organizational objectives, and measurable impact on organizational goals.

Concerns/Downsides

Some of the opponents of this kind of development activity have voiced these concerns:

Concern: 20 percent is enough time to have ideas and get started on projects but not necessarily enough time to do them well or finish and carry them through.

Overcome it: Not only can good ideas continue to be developed to implementation, one small step at a time with persistence, but it's also important to remember that good ideas that benefit the organization can be moved out of the 20 percent category and into real production. Capitalize on the opportunity and move faster to optimizing its benefits!

Concern: Many companies don't like spending money on R&D (research and development) in the first place and would hate the idea of employees spending time on things that aren't immediately productive.

Overcome it: Using existing resources for additional R&D is a low-cost, low-risk way to get more innovation from what you already have. Think about it as squeezing more value from your current assets!

Concern: Some managers cling to monthly profit figures for dear life and operate with a short- versus long-term focus and would lack the vision or patience to support this kind of idea.

Overcome it: While it is hard to change short-term biased mindsets, sometimes showing small wins and making a cumulative case for the benefits and value will help even the most stubborn critics find it difficult to ignore facts on the ground.

Concern: Some employees aren't interested in creativity and don't have the drive to pursue innovative side projects properly. They just want to do their regular jobs and take home their wages with a minimum of fuss—they aren't passionate about their work.

Overcome it: Use the self-assessment in this chapter (Figure 11-1) to see whether it's a good fit for you and your staff. Start with those who are ready and help those who are not ready move toward the creative approach with incremental steps. Also, if employees lack passion for their job, consider whether they are not well matched with their current roles and whether there is a better, more fitting way to help optimize their skills and strengths.

Concern: We shouldn't use Google as a role model without considering that it has a unique mix of people who are at once intensely ambitious, creative, and very adaptable to hierarchy and benchmarks (as shown by their SATs and Ivy League/Stanford/Berkeley credentials). This wouldn't work in other environments with a different mix of employees.

Overcome it: Are there companies whose culture won't support this? Or, stated another way, is there prerequisite work required to change the culture somewhat so that it is supported? It's hard to say. Sometimes it's best to "Think Globally, Act Locally," as the saying goes. Nothing is perfect, but if the payoff is worthy, we should give it our best effort and start from where we are with a grassroots effort to make the change we want. The conditions will never be exactly right, and it's a shame to miss out on opportunities by waiting for perfection.

Concern: Fear and risk aversion. What will ensure that employees really apply themselves and don't waste time surfing the Internet instead?

Overcome it: Advocates of this system overwhelmingly describe it as operating in a culture of trust and mutual accountability. For the best results, you need to be trusting and trustworthy before attempting such a development approach. Risk-averse or low-trust organizations (or leaders) may not be comfortable enough to allow for this type of investment. However, there is hope: You can take it slow, approach the plan incrementally (think baby steps), and give it time to accumulate small wins that build trust. This approach can build trust in a spiral of mutual growth (see Figure 11-2).

Figure 11-2 ▪ Trust-Building Spiral

Concern: Some people will still use the time to surf the web (they'll call it research) while others may become obsessed and overshoot the 20 percent mark, working on their side project too much of the time and not getting their regular work done.

Overcome it: Most employees would feel so honored, lucky, and grateful for this freedom to create that they will be extra motivated to protect it. In fact, companies who've tried this method report that employees are more motivated and productive during their nonzone time because they know that they will have the chance to drill into the ideas and concerns that arise during daily work later on, during zone time. Manage performance as you would with any other work. Deal directly with employees who are not aligned with goals and deadlines by providing timely constructive feedback and performance improvement coaching.

Concern: Companies are afraid of it because they feel as if they'll lose control of their employees' projects. Bosses like to know exactly what employees are doing and approve of every move. With the 20 percent time, one day out of a five-day workweek could be spent working on something the boss doesn't believe in at all. That's scary for bosses.

Overcome it: As mentioned above, not only will your organization benefit from the fruits of employees' labor from zone time, but it will also benefit from the added commitment, engagement, and productivity that these employees will have during their regular work hours as a result of being allowed the autonomy to be creative and the appreciation of the freedom they are given.

Concern: Leaders may think that employees don't have enough work to do if they have the time to engage in this kind of activity. It may be perceived as a negative reflection on the employee's productivity or level of output.

Overcome it: There is no question that garnering leadership's understanding of the concept and support of it will help avoid this kind of problem in the first place. The more you can communicate the purpose and intended outcomes of the project to leaders, the better chance you will have of gaining their support and avoiding suspicion. If you simply engage in this type of development without "selling it" to the organization, the more room you leave for wrong interpretation.

RESOURCES

Constine, J. (2012, January 7). *4 Facebook Employees Built A Working Demo Of Timeline In One Night*. Retrieved from http://m.techcrunch .com/2012/01/05/timeline-built-in-a-day/?utm_source=feedburner&

Mediratta, B., as told to J. Bick. (2007, October 21). The Google Way: Give Engineers Room. *The New York Times*. Retrieved from http:// www.nytimes.com/2007/10/21/jobs/21pre.html?_r=1

Pink, D. (2010). *Drive: The Surprising Truth About What Motivates Us*. New York: Riverhead Books.

Segall, L. (2011, March 9). *Hackathon Recipe: Insomnia + Red Bull = New Apps*. Retrieved from http://www.stumbleupon.com/su/1Qqvzr/ money.cnn.com/2011/03/09/technology/hackathons/index.htm

Twitter Engineering. (2010, October 22). *Hack Week*. Retrieved from http://engineering.twitter.com/2010/10/hack-week.html

Chapter 12

GETTING SOCIAL: SOCIAL LEARNING TOOLS

WHAT IS IT?

Social learning, or Learning 2.0, is a general name given to multiple collaborative online tools for sharing knowledge, building relationships, and interacting with content and with other members of the online community. These tools allow learners to learn independently, more quickly, and more efficiently, and to be more productive and effective as a result. Most of the content in these systems is user generated and user rated for interest, relevance, and helpfulness. In this chapter, we will focus on the tools most commonly used by organizations for learning purposes: wikis and social networking tools such as discussion boards, blogs, video uploading platforms, and podcasting.

Wiki

A wiki is a website for collaborative creation and uploading of content. The wiki pages are webpages interlinked via a web browser that allows all users to edit any page or create new pages within the wiki. However, it's possible to set up a wiki with varying editorial permission levels. Typically, different pages can be linked to each other by topic associations, which makes searching on a wiki intuitive and easy. The name for this tool comes from the Hawaiian word *wiki* meaning "fast" or "quick." A wiki helps organizations develop and leverage their collective intelligence.

Workplace Online Social Networking Tools

Online social networking systems can take various forms and are similar to the popular, freely available social sites you may be familiar with already such as YouTube, Facebook, LinkedIn, and Ning. They are usually private and only open to employees of the organization. Furthermore, social networking systems also include blogs and discussion boards where community members can discuss common issues and comment on each other's uploaded content. Employees can use these enterprise social networking tools to share information, opinions, ideas, content, thoughts, answers, and best practices easily and quickly. They can also form groups and communities of interest around business issues or topics of common interest, which not only facilitates the exchange of information but also builds networks of interpersonal connections across the organization.

Sun Microsystems employees use an enterprise social learning site called Social Learning eXchange (SLX), which is kind of like a corporate YouTube, to let staff record, post, and share a wide variety of content and media. In their book, *The 2020 Workplace*, Jeanne C. Meister and Karie Willyerd (2010) share an example of how this kind of system supports just-in-time employee development by telling the story of an employee who downloads a sales training video or podcast to his iPod and views it on his morning train ride to work. He then reads the comments posted by his peers telling about how they tailored the approach with their clients and what results they experienced. When he arrives at work, this employee is ready to serve clients thanks to the learning content and the social interaction offered via the SLX, and all before he even got to work (Meister and Willyerd, 2010).

Video and Podcasting

Employees can watch or listen to a wide range of instructional videos and podcasts either via public platforms or enterprise systems. They can also upload content easily for others to watch or listen to. And employees can rate and comment on this content, thereby interacting with the content creators as well as other users, around the organization or around the world. IBM uses podcasts to circulate knowledge to a workforce that is dispersed across many time zones instead of using costly international conference calls, for example.

There are many overlaps between this section and both the chapter on self-directed learning (chapter 2) and the chapter on videos and podcasts (chapter 10). The former explains how using these resources as the viewer/listener can develop employees, and the latter explains how creating and uploading the content can also serve as a good employee development method. Therefore, it will not be necessary to discuss this option in specific detail in this chapter, as that would be redundant.

WHO SHOULD TRY IT?

Every employee with access to an Internet connection and a computer can benefit from social learning as a development tool. Regardless of their levels of expertise or tenure, all employees can benefit from sharing information, creating connections, and getting access to the cross-cutting organizational body of expertise and knowledge of other employees, anywhere, anytime.

New employees can gain information easily and quickly to help them onboard more smoothly. Seasoned employees can discuss and learn from their peers across the organization and expand their network of internal contacts. And subject matter experts can easily document and share their knowledge of organizational products, services, processes, procedures, workarounds and shortcuts, and systems. And all employees can share expertise and intelligence gathered from outside the organization such as vendor information, industry news and knowledge, client needs and feedback, and competitive insights.

Managers and leaders can use these tools to improve team and organizational performance and gain insight into key employee concerns and interests. They can also use social learning tools for building and developing teams as well as providing performance support mechanisms to teams and individual staff members.

HOW DOES IT BENEFIT THE LEARNER?

Social learning benefits the learner in several ways:

- Credible information and advice (peer-judged by other users). Wikis and online networking tools allow users to rate content or answer polling questions. This functionality allows community members to assess the usefulness and relevance of content based on the statistics associated with it, such as how highly it's been ranked by other members or what other users reported about it in polls.
- Just-in-time, fast, and targeted learning opportunities. Information is at the learners' fingertips from wherever they work, whenever they need it. They can search and locate exactly what they need to know at the moment they need to know it rather than waiting for a more formal learning opportunity to arise.
- Sense of ownership of learning process. Because the content is user generated and interactive, learners can feel more empowered to actively engage in and own their learning experience.
- Wide access to the full organizational network. Learners can tap into all areas of the organization, cross-functionally and in various locations. They can form personal connections with experts and leaders in ways that aren't as feasible or likely in more traditional learning methods. This access gives them better and wider resources for learning information and skills. It also creates more, better, and broader relationships that help them perform and collaborate better in their current as well as future roles.

Other benefits to the learner include:

- Creativity and new thinking about business issues and challenges.
- Increased job satisfaction.
- Higher engagement.
- Skill and knowledge development.
- Career development.

- Positive attitude toward learning, which leads to learning more efficiently.

HOW DOES IT BENEFIT THE ORGANIZATION?

The organization also benefits from social learning:

- Performance improvement and support. Individual employees can perform more effectively by learning from others' mistakes and successes through the social learning tools. They have faster access to high-quality content and knowledge sharing. You can support performance by uploading flashcards, FAQ pages, checklists, and best practices on a wiki, which helps with employee learning and knowledge sharing. Social networking systems can serve as instant, on-the-job, just-in-time job aids because employees anywhere, anytime, can search for answers to questions and get the right expert's advice and insight quickly, even if they've never met the expert.
- Reduced learning costs and increased efficiencies. Social learning allows you to reduce the costs to develop and deliver learning content when compared with traditional learning vehicles. It also helps streamline the information sharing and learning process and allows you to introduce efficiencies and savings through collaboration. Finally, using existing social media instead of custom-designed ones can reduce the up-front costs associated with introducing Learning 2.0 systems.
- Reduced errors. Employees have access to just-in-time, quality information and answers to their questions. They have access to expert-generated content that helps them perform in a more efficient way and reduces their likelihood of making mistakes.
- Improved organizational performance. The enterprise becomes more nimble by the creation of learning communities and a learning culture. The collaboration also

creates a more highly engaged workforce. Decision-making capabilities are improved by the timely access to broad input from multiple stakeholders and the ability to reach consensus with more complete deliberation via the social learning tools. There is even a greater likelihood of innovation and breakthroughs on tough business problems by using the social learning tools to "crowd-source" knowledge, expertise, and creative problem resolution. The organization's various components can be more easily aligned, and business issues can be resolved faster, thereby improving profits and customer satisfaction.

- Improved onboarding process. You can upload content from various onboarding training programs on the wiki for new employees to review and comment on. New employees can ask questions and read comments on the social networking platforms to further expand their knowledge and skills in their new roles.

- Knowledge management. You can capture the tacit knowledge of employees in wiki pages and blogs. Especially important is capturing the knowledge of Baby Boomers and highly experienced or specialized employees so that it is recorded and available to newer employees. The seasoned employees can create content that can later be used by new hires as well as other employees to gain knowledge and solve problems, even after the content creators have left the organization.

- Improved launch of new products or organizational initiatives. Subject matter experts (SMEs) update content relevant to a new product or initiative in the wiki and generate a discussion in the comments employees leave about this information. More discussion can be seeded and nurtured in the social networking platforms. This interaction builds greater awareness for these new products or initiatives and helps employees reduce uncertainty and confusion by getting input and answers to their questions immediately.

- Performance support for the organization's client-facing workforce. Employees who are "out in the field"—in sales, customer service, or other client-facing roles—often need experts' input to help resolve client or product/service issues quickly. They may encounter these quandaries when they are not in their own offices and cannot simply walk over to another employee to ask questions or get support. These employees can quickly access the wiki or social networking tools to get information just in time from SMEs. This functionality can greatly improve their ability to market and sell, train new sales and service staff, and serve prospects and clients.

- Improved relevance and accuracy of documentation. Because wikis and social learning content can be continuously updated by all the members of the user community, organizations can have better assurances that employees have the latest knowledge on the Learning 2.0 platforms.

- Increased collaboration among geographically dispersed employees. Dispersed team members can discuss and learn even complex concepts using a wiki because they can share textual and graphic information and discuss it, in real time, like using a virtual whiteboard in a virtual conference room. Also, wikis and social networking tools increase collaboration and communication among internal experts and other employees through the comment function and the discussion boards.

- Continuous learning culture. Employees gain ongoing access to subject matter experts with whom they may not have otherwise connected (especially in large organizations). Members of online communities identify experts who write wiki pages and blogs that help meet the learning needs of the community. Employees can tap into the knowledge of the experts anytime and can easily get credible, varied, expert answers to questions they have, in real time.

191

- Improved cohesion of disparate workforce. Employees who are in disparate geographical locations can connect via these online social networking systems to share information such as wiki articles, blog posts, and media files. They can form relationships via chats, comment threads, and discussion boards that connect them with other members of the wider community within the organization.

WHAT COMPETENCIES AND SKILLS CAN IT DEVELOP?

The subject matter for the interactions and content creation on social learning platforms varies greatly, and so do the competencies that can be developed by using this development method. Here are some ideas:

- Written communication—those who upload content can practice and develop their writing skills.
- Partnering—because social networking tools encourage employees to engage collaboratively across boundaries, build alliances, and find common ground with a wide variety of stakeholders, this is a great vehicle for developing their partnering competency.
- Interpersonal skills—through the social interactions on the organization's social learning tools (especially in comments and on discussion boards), employees can develop their skills of being tactful and sensitive, treating others with respect, and considering the needs and feelings of different people in different situations.

HOW DOES IT WORK?

How to Prepare

In preparation for development via social learning tools, answer the following questions:

- What are the desired outcomes for using these development tools?

- What measures will be used to assess the learner's progress and success?
- What might you or your organization need to do to ensure that this kind of investment of employee time and effort is well spent?
- How will you or your organization ensure that you communicate the purpose and desired outcomes of this type of learning?
- What technology is needed? What other resources are required?
- How will the learner record and report an account of progress and learning as well as accomplishments?
- How will you celebrate progress and goal achievement?

Ways to Track Progress and Results

- This type of development method provides ongoing, just-in-time opportunities to learn new information and create new connections. It isn't likely that employees will need to quantify the number of pages they read or commented on.
- If employees' developmental goal is to improve their writing skills, then it would be appropriate to measure the number, length, and popularity/usefulness (through ratings, number of views, and so on) of the content they generate.
- If the goal is to increase cross-functional connections, you could measure the number of new connections made each month, and the number of interactions or the number of times employees comment on content and have discussions with other employees in specific areas of the business they wanted to target.
- Other ideas:

_____

_____

_____

_____

_____

Implementation Tips

Social learning is here to stay. Face the fact—social learning is not going away. It's going to grow in prevalence and importance, so we might as well take the leap and embrace it.

Change will happen. Social learning is in its infancy, and it will continue to evolve.

Social learning is not enough. Blend it with other development methods—social learning is complementary, not meant to replace other methods.

Take baby steps. Avoid the all-or-nothing approach—phase it in slowly, incrementally.

Help it grow. Create some seed content and get some early commenters to get the conversation started. This grassroots effort will build momentum and lead to culture change over time.

The learners are your target. Maintain your focus on the learners, not the system, the content, or the bells and whistles. It must serve the learners' needs and address their expectations, or they won't find it valuable and won't use it.

Listen to users. Ask them questions and be open to changing what you're doing along the way.

Balance flexibility and control. Strike the delicate balance between allowing full freedom for the open-space "sandbox" experience and measuring metrics so rigidly that it inhibits or restricts the ease of participation, collaboration, and users' interaction with content and each other.

Required Resources and Supports

Technology systems. You will need to research the latest vendor offerings in the market as this type of technology is constantly updating and evolving. Know that there are free tools, inexpensive tools, and top-of-the-line and costly tools to choose from. The bottom line is that online social interaction and content sharing cannot happen without an online platform that supports it. There are also bandwidth and firewall considerations to keep in mind. A good book to get you started is Tony Bingham and Marcia Conner's *The New Social Learning: A Guide to Transforming Organizations Through Social Media* (2010).

Also check out Meister and Willyerd's *The 2020 Workplace: How Innovative Companies Attract, Develop, and Keep Tomorrow's Employees Today* (2010), and Jane Bozarth's *Social Media for Trainers: Techniques for Enhancing and Extending Learning (Essential Tools Resource;* 2010).

A good summary of some considerations and options is offered by *The Learning Generalist* (2010a, 2010b).

Concerns/Downsides

Some of the opponents of this kind of development activity have voiced these concerns:

Concern: It's expensive to build these kinds of systems. It's not in my budget, and I don't think I can prove the ROI for this kind of expenditure.

Overcome it: Similar to video and podcasting tools, it can be expensive if you choose the Rolls-Royce version of the system that is on the market, but you can also offer many of the benefits of social learning to your organization for little to no up-front costs by using some of the widely available free tools and working within their existing parameters and constraints. Also, because this can be a grassroots effort that builds slowly and gains momentum as it grows, you can start small and cheap and then make a stronger case for ROI once the system is in place and you can quantify results.

Concern: Users may generate offensive or irrelevant "junk" content that may cause a potential misuse of these tools or possibly violate the security policy.

Overcome it: You can avoid this problem by adding a moderation layer in the Learning 2.0 systems. Administrators, system "champions," and community moderators can moderate and delete the junk and irrelevant user-generated content from the social networking and social bookmarking systems. If you want further protection of systems from any security violations, you could introduce access control and page locking measures.

Concern: Low user participation. What if users don't collaborate and generate the content required for the Learning 2.0 platform to be effective?

Overcome it: It is said that only 5 percent of an organization's workforce creates content, so this is a valid concern that can be successfully overcome. You'll need to help users follow an example by seeding these systems with some helpful, relevant content. It's easier to follow suit than to start from scratch.

You should identify and implement systems that end users consider relevant and useful to their critical job functions and responsibilities. For example, if users can easily search and find "help" content in the wiki for on-the-job help, they will tend to return to it more frequently.

Identify a community manager to seed and curate relevant content in the online communities. Effective wiki "champions" and community moderators from among the users can help further drive up user participation. Finally, ensure that your performance management and reward structure doesn't somehow discourage users from generating content.

Concern: Some employees will enjoy these tools so much that they will spend a disproportionately large amount of time on them. This will prevent them from meeting their performance goals and job priorities.

Overcome it: Just like any other potential derailment and distraction, this too must be one that is actively monitored and managed by the employee's supervisor. For great performance to take place, employees must know what their managers expect of them, know how their performance will be measured, and have ongoing feedback conversations to keep them on track. Active and effective ongoing performance management (which is assumed as the standard with or without Learning 2.0 systems in place) allows the organization, and its employees, to stay effective, productive, and successful.

Concern: No benchmarks or performance measurements. Learning 2.0 systems do not lend themselves to tracking and measuring employee learning like traditional instructor-led and e-learning platforms do.

Overcome it: While you can't measure learning directly, there are ways you can measure it indirectly. When employees add comments to content in wikis, blogs, online communities, videos, and podcasts, you could qualitatively assess the knowledge they gained and their level of expertise. Furthermore, you could assess users through community polls and surveys. Additionally, users can rate content in the social learning systems (using the stars or thumbs-up ratings embedded in wikis, blogs, and discussion boards, for example), which can further indicate interest and preferences and help assess the quality of the online experts.

Concern: Format can vary among departments and locations. Because users generate the content, it's hard to ensure format uniformity across the organization.

Overcome it: Is format uniformity important? If users are uploading content they find relevant, and rating the relevance of content their peers create, then the content is useful and helpful to them as it is. Don't worry too much about making it adhere to a preconceived, rigid format.

CASE STUDY

Electronic Arts (EA), an interactive game company, offers a social networking platform to its 9,000 employees. EA People, as it's called, helps employees share information and connect with each other. The employees create a personal profile—much like they do on Facebook or LinkedIn—that lets them describe their skills, interests, and experiences using searchable preloaded options for ease of searching. The system also is integrating the company's wiki and article library so that the content is linked to the authors and the authors' profiles. This helps create more personal connections between experts and users.

In the fiercely competitive and fast-moving industry that is gaming, there is increasing pressure on EA's staff to assimilate new knowledge fast and work collaboratively with team members to deliver better and better products as soon as possible. The company also continues to experience growth and faces the need to onboard new hires effectively and quickly. One of the biggest benefits of the social networking tool to EA staff members is the way it enables them to network with a wider array of other employees to find colleagues who have worked on similar problems to the one they're facing so they can learn from others' experience and decrease their learning curve. They can quickly find employees with particular jobs or talents or experiences and get the answers they need in real time.

EA decided to release the tool quietly onto the corporate intranet when it was ready instead of widely marketing it. The culture is one where there is resistance to adopting new corporate applications because employees feel they are forced on them. Therefore, by allowing the tool to be discovered rather than pushed, it built a grassroots core of users that quickly became viral through word of mouth. The internal champion seeded the tool first by inviting 50 employees who were active users of the company's Facebook group to join and invite their friends. Within two and a half months, EA People had 2,500 employee profile pages created, and within a few more months, 3,500 employees—over one third of the entire staff—had pages.

EA continues to survey users as well as follow trends and add new features to the system. The ultimate goal is to foster collaboration, increase innovation, and help staff deliver faster, better games to the market. While the social networking site can't directly deliver these results, it feeds them indirectly by providing new and seasoned employees with a convenient and quick way to find information and expertise in other employees so that they can innovate, create, and solve problems better and faster. EA People averages 200 hits per day and 100 people searches per day, showing that it is useful and relevant. It definitely enhances networking and information sharing and facilitates onboarding (Microsoft Case Studies, 2011).

RESOURCES

Bingham, T., and M. Conner. (2010). *The New Social Learning: A Guide to Transforming Organizations Through Social Media*. Alexandria, VA: American Society for Training and Development and San Fancisco: Berrett-Koehler.

Bozarth, J. (2010). *Social Media for Trainers: Techniques for Enhancing and Extending Learning (Essential Tools Resource)*. San Francisco: Pfeiffer.

Davidove, E., and C. Mindrum. (2010, March). Verifying Virtual Value. *Chief Learning Officer*, pp. 28–31, 48.

Dublin, L. (2010, March). Formalizing Informal Learning. *Chief Learning Officer*, pp. 20–23.

Klapper, B. (2010, March). From Entropy to Excellence. *Chief Learning Officer*, pp. 36–39.

The Learning Generalist. (2010a, June 27). *Here Are 6 Social Learning Platforms You Can Enable "On-Demand."* Retrieved from http://www.learninggeneralist.com/2010/06/here-are-6-social-learning-platforms.html

The Learning Generalist. (2010b, November 2). *Understanding the Tools of the Social Learning Landscape*. Retrieved from http://www.learninggeneralist.com/2010/11/understanding-tools-of-social-learning.html

Meister, J.C., and K. Willyerd. (2010). *The 2020 Workplace: How Innovative Companies Attract, Develop, and Keep Tomorrow's Employees Today*. New York: HarperBusiness.

Microsoft Case Studies. (2011). *Electronic Arts Embraces Social Networking to Create Better Games on Tight Timelines*. Posted May 18, 2009. Retrieved from http://65.55.21.250/caseStudies/Case_Study_Detail.aspx?casestudyid=4000004267

Miller, R. (2010, August 30). *Enterprise Social Networking: 10 Applications You Need to Know About*. Retrieved from http://www.focus.com/briefs/enterprise-social-networking-10-applications-you-need-know-a/

Sherman, B. (2010, March). The Social LMS. *Chief Learning Officer*, pp. 32–35.

Sontakey, A. (2009). Compress Your Learning Curve: Improve Enterprise Learning Through Collaboration and Knowledge Sharing. *Infosys SET-Labs Briefings*, 7(3). Retrieved from http://www.infosys.com/infosys-labs/publications/setlabs-briefings/Pages/compress-your-learning-curve.aspx

SUMMARY—NOW WHAT?

TYING IT ALL TOGETHER

The idea behind this book was to share lots of different ideas with you about how to develop employees outside the classroom and on a tight budget. I hope that you gained many insights and inspirations to start thinking about ways to leverage the resources already at your disposal to create unlimited potential with your existing staff. By developing their current skills to the next level, you can help employees bring greater value to the organization and become even stronger players on your team. By creating opportunities for your employees to grow into new skill sets and competencies, you can help them stay motivated, engaged, and loyal to you and the organization that has invested in their growth.

Whether you have decided to implement simpler methods like self-directed learning or mentoring, or more demanding methods like innovation/creativity zones or social learning, one thing's for sure: It's important to take your dream, your ideas, and your vision, and make them a reality.

NEXT STEPS

What will you do to ensure that employee development is thriving in your organization or on your team? How will you take some of the ideas that this book inspired in you and make them come to life? What will it take? Take a few minutes and write down what your vision is for the next year in terms of employee development. Be as vivid and descriptive in your language as possible.

_____

_____

_____

_____

_____

_____

Now, decide what broad, overarching goals will help make that vision a reality. Remember, write them in a SMART way.

Goal 1: _____

_____

_____

_____

_____

Goal 2: _____

_____

_____

_____

_____

Goal 3: _____

_____

_____

_____

_____

Now think about the specific activities that will make up each goal. What actions must you take to achieve each goal?

_____

_____

_____

_____

_____

_____

_____

_____

_____

_____

Be sure to transfer these activities, goals, and vision into your permanent planning system (your calendar, your Outlook or Lotus Notes, or wherever you keep yourself organized). Schedule actions you must take in the next two weeks to get started, so that you don't lose your momentum. And go make the changes you have envisioned to improve employee development options for your employees. I would love to hear about your successes and challenges—please drop me a note about it at halelly@talentgrow.com.

Happy learning!

INDEX

ABOUT THE AUTHOR

Halelly Azulay is a workplace learning professional specializing in guiding people and organizations of all types and sizes to peak performance. She brings 20 years of professional experience in the fields of workplace learning and communication to corporate, government, regulatory, nonprofit, and academic clients.

Halelly is the president of TalentGrow, a consulting company focused on developing leaders and teams to improve the human side of work. TalentGrow specializes in leadership, communication skills, team building, facilitation, coaching, and emotional intelligence. Halelly works with all organizational levels including C-level leaders, frontline managers, and individual contributors.

Halelly works with organizations such as PricewaterhouseCoopers, Booz Allen Hamilton, the Food and Drug Administration, Office of Naval Research, FINRA (formerly NASD), and the University of Maryland among others. She is past president of the board of the award-winning metro D.C. chapter of the American Society for Training and Development (ASTD), where she served in various leadership roles from 2005 to 2010. Halelly was selected to judge the 2009 and 2010 Apollo Awards for excellence in employee development and is a sought after speaker at conferences and meetings for various organizations about leadership, employee development, and communication.

Halelly is a contributing author to numerous books, such as *The Insider's Guide to Supervising Government Employees*, *The Pfeiffer Annual: Training*, *The Pfeiffer Annual: Consulting*, and *The Trainer's Warehouse Book of Games: Fun and Energizing Ways to Enhance Learning*, as well as articles and blogs.

Halelly lives in a suburb of Washington, D.C., with her husband, David, their two boys, and two cats. She enjoys exercising, learning about nutrition, dancing salsa, and experiencing the food and music of other cultures. She invites readers to email her at halelly@talentgrow.com.